Pay for College

Without Sacrificing Your

Retirement

Pay for College

Without Sacrificing Your

Retirement

A Guide to Your Financial Future

Tim Higgins

Bay Tree Publishing
Point Richmond, California

Design and composition by mlTrees

Library of Congress Cataloging-in-Publication Data

Higgins, Tim, 1976-
  Pay for college without sacrificing your retirement : a guide to your financial future / by Tim Higgins.
      p. cm.
  Includes bibliographical references and index.
    Summary: "Examines the cost of college within the context of a family financial plan; financial aid; academic, athletic and need-based scholarships; tax sheltered savings plans such as 529s; potential help from grandparents; and the use of business assets, loans, home equity, and retirement savings"--Provided by publisher.
  ISBN 978-0-9720021-8-9
  1. College costs--United States. 2. Student aid--United States. 3. Finance, Personal--United States. I. Title.

  LB2342.H488 2008
  378.3--dc22
                          2008010376

Contents

Preface

It was late summer, just before I was about to begin my senior year in high school. We were driving back from Wesleyan University after having toured the campus and met with the baseball coach. My father said something to me that changed my way of thinking about college and opened my eyes to issues that I didn't even know existed. About fifteen minutes after leaving the campus and following a brief moment of silence, he said, "Tim, if you would like to go to Wesleyan, we will do whatever it takes."

Pause.

Silence.

I didn't know how to react. "Do whatever it takes." Why would my dad say that to me, and why now? I had been on numerous college tours with my parents, including road trips through Massachusetts, Connecticut, Pennsylvania, upstate New York, and Vermont, but my father had never made a comment like that.

My first panicked thoughts ran something like this: "Oh no, is paying for college going to be a problem? This is the kind of statement you make when you don't have the money. Am I going to be a financial burden on my parents? What sacrifice am I asking them to make? Wow! I thought paying for college wasn't an issue, at least, until now I didn't. Almost everyone I know is going to college. Do other families have the same issue? I think my parents do pretty well with their business. I have never noticed us having financial issues. Am I missing something? I wish they had mentioned it before. I don't have to go to such an expensive school."

Until that moment there had been no question about whether I was going to college; it was what everyone did, what my parents wanted, and why I had been padding my "resume" with all kinds of things I didn't really want to do (like joining the math team).

My second set of thoughts were quite different. "What did my parents see in this school that they didn't see in the others? They must really have liked it, and they must have been impressed for my father to say something like that. I thought it was nice, but there must be something different, something special about it that makes it worthwhile, even if some sacrifices have to be made. If that's how they feel, perhaps going here would be the best thing for me, and, on top of that, it would make them happy."

Yes, all those thoughts really did rush through my head in a couple of minutes. In the end, I still didn't know what to say or how to react, and I was afraid to ask about money issues. I had never discussed money with my parents, and I didn't know how to begin.

I know that not every family goes through the exact same experience that my family and I did. But I do know, for a fact, having spoken with hundreds of parents, that there are two common themes that many share.

1. Students are usually unaware of the financial impact of the cost of college. To take it one step further, they wouldn't be able to comprehend it even if they were aware. They have no idea how easy or hard it may be to pay back $10,000, $20,000, or $50,000 in student loans. They have no idea how much monthly discretionary cash flow you have. They are clueless (and you may be, too) if you are on track for your retirement. What most do know is that almost all their friends will be going, and that they want to, too.

I believe it is healthy for parents to have financial discussions with their children. It means that both parents and children have the same information and together they can define what is realistic; it also reduces stress in the long run. Moreover, if children do not start learning about how to handle finances in high school, when will they learn? High schools don't teach courses on money management. Some colleges do, but for students who don't get this exposure, there are plenty of credit card companies soliciting students on and off campus that would be happy to enroll them in some real-life lessons.

Unfortunately, many parents have never discussed finances with their children. When it then comes time to selecting a college, their seventeen- and eighteen-year-old children are making

$180,000 decisions for the whole family. Is this, or could this be, your situation?

2. A lot of parents will do "whatever it takes," just as my father said he would. In fact, I know that many parents care more about paying for a college degree for their children than about any other financial goal. They see a college education as perhaps the most important ingredient in providing for their children's future success. This intense emotional charge makes it difficult to make a wise decision. As any salesman will tell you, people buy based on emotions, not facts or logic, and colleges (as businesses) reap the benefits.

Thus, this highly charged do-whatever-it-takes attitude leads many families to make poor decisions when it comes to selecting a college. I hope this book will both help you cut down the total cost of college and, more importantly, encourage you to step back, evaluate your resources, and develop a financial game plan before you commit to writing five-figure checks every year.

I did apply to Wesleyan and was accepted. Soon to follow was the financial aid package that indicated that "doing whatever it takes" was indeed a daunting prospect. At first, we were not offered any type of financial assistance from the school. Interestingly enough, my parents kept this fact from me. I was completely unaware of the financial aid process until the evening we received a phone call from the Wesleyan baseball coach.

This was my second eye-opening precollege experience. The coach called, but he didn't ask to speak to me. After my father concluded his brief discussion and hung up, my mother and I wanted to know the scoop. What was that all about?

My father explained that the coach wanted to find out if we had received our financial aid package from the college. My father said that we had. The coach also wanted to know if we were satisfied with the package. My father indicated that the zero dollars we were offered in assistance didn't seem to make paying the $35,000 annual bill much easier. Needless to say, the conversation concluded with the coach promising to place a call to the financial aid department on our behalf.

Within a couple of weeks we received a new financial aid package that looked a lot different from the first. This time I was offered grants and scholarships, a work-study job, and subsidized student loans, which meant I could borrow money at 0 percent interest while a student. Free money plus a job on campus plus student loans at 0 percent—this was a lot better.

Wow, that was easy; a phone call from a coach and my college costs dropped by thousands of dollars per year!

As an eighteen-year-old I thought that almost all families must have similar interactions with colleges. I made the naive assumption that everyone applies for financial aid and then works with the college to get a satisfactory package. Well, when I finally started college and began talking to other students, I found out that I was in the minority. I was one of the few who had actually had the financial aid letter amended. In addition, I was one of the few with a work-study job, one of the few with student loans, and one of the few who actually applied for financial aid.

Today Wesleyan costs around $45,000 a year, and according to CollegeBoard.com, out of the 720 freshmen who enrolled in the fall of 2007, only 397, or 55 percent, even applied for financial aid.

Apparently, almost half the families sending their children off to Wesleyan think the yield per hour of completing financial aid forms is not worth their time. In my work as a financial advisor, I see enough to know that cutting a check for $45,000 is not an easy thing for anyone to do. You would think more families would at least ask for help.

While I hope that every high school graduate who wishes to attend college manages to do so, and has a great experience to boot, this book is addressed primarily to parents. Why? Because a large majority of the parents I work with are sacrificing their retirements in order to meet the extremely high cost of college.

My approach to college financial planning has two goals: one, to help you provide your child with the best education possible; and two, to save you money along the way because you are going to need it not too many years later. The biggest obstacle to your retirement may be the large checks you are writing for the four to twelve years your children are in college. This is why it's so important to take the time to look at your financial goals and make the effort to reduce the amount of money you pay for your children's college educations. Ultimately, you'll preserve a larger portion of your retirement savings.

1

You Can Borrow for College—Not Retirement

Picture a timeline that represents your past, present, and future working career. Let's say it begins when you were in your early twenties and will last until the standard retirement age of sixty-five. Something very significant happens at the end of this timeline.

Your salary stops. For the rest of your life you will have to pay the utility bills, make car payments, and finance your vacations through your combined savings, social security, and pension income. Do you have enough?

Whatever conclusions you reach regarding your future, I can assure you that the picture will be significantly affected by how you pay for college.

Let's look at a scenario for a family of four that will be sending two children off to elite private colleges. The total cost of eight years of private college (assuming it will take only eight years and completely ignoring inflation) could easily be more than $360,000 (eight years at $45,000 per year) paid after taxes. Those in the 28 percent tax bracket will have to earn $500,000 in order to meet this cost.

Even if you are planning to send your children to state, or public, colleges, where the costs are far lower, the important thing to remember is that how you pay for college is directly tied to the amount of money you will have at retirement. Every dollar you save on college costs and instead invest in your retirement will be worth more to you down the road.

If you are fifty now and plan to retire at sixty-five, your current investments will be worth about four times what they are today at an average return of 10 percent per year. I think of this as "The Rule of Four." Even though some portion of that growth will be offset by inflation, and even if you earn somewhat less than 10 percent, the growth in your retirement savings can be significant over a fifteen-year period. The $3,000 you save today could be worth $12,000 for your retirement, and $30,000 could be worth $120,000. Keeping the Rule of Four in mind can motivate you to be more proactive in seeking out savings while figuring out how to pay for a child's college.

Your Biggest Financial Goals

For most American families, the three most important financial goals are (1) owning a home, (2) educating their children, and (3) saving enough to retire.

For most people, these three are connected. How we handle our home equity and mortgage may be tied to how, and how much, we pay for our children's college educations. Whatever assets remain after college expenses, then contribute to retirement. This is where I want to add a strong reminder:

> You can borrow for college, but you
> can't borrow for retirement.

You may want to repeat that phrase to yourself a few times because it holds the key to much of the substance in this book.

Let's now return to the scenario of spending a total of $360,000 to send two children to college and explore a few other issues. How much did you pay for your house when you bought it? Your estimated college expenses might easily be in the same ballpark. How many years do you have to pay off your home? For most of us, it's thirty years. Do you want to be paying off your children's college for thirty years? How old would you be when you finish? Do you still want to be paying for your children's education when you are in your seventies or eighties?

I would bet that when you bought your home, you felt it was the major purchase (and buying decision) in your life. Well, looking at the numbers, I'm suggesting you think of paying for college in the same light. Now ask yourself at what age you are thinking of retiring. How close to that retirement age will you be when your last child graduates? And, when he or she does graduate, how financially ready will you be for retirement?

I don't want to scare you by addressing retirement and college at the same time, but I do want you to understand how important it is to look at these issues simultaneously, because they are linked. By figuring out the details of your retirement, you will be able to calculate what kind of college contributions are realistic for you.

Let's go back to the timeline for a second. Assuming that you will be making payments to colleges while you are in your forties and fifties, you can see that not much time separates your last college payment from your retirement. Since very few families will have a school or organization subsidizing 100 percent of their college costs, most will need to work hard and budget carefully to pay for college. The kind of comprehensive financial planning outlined in this book can make a huge difference in your financial future as you go through that process.

Planning through the Eyes of a CFO

The first step in developing a long-term financial plan is to start thinking of your household as a mini-business. On a regular basis, it has income coming in, expenses going out, and excess cash invested with varying returns, and each year you hope to be in a better financial position than the last. Like some businesses, there are households that overextend themselves and fall behind. Others make good decisions, use their resources well, and grow.

Most large businesses have one person who is dedicated full time to handling the finances. This person's title is chief financial officer, or CFO, and it is his or her job to make a company more profitable by handling its finances efficiently. This can mean reducing costs or making wise investment decisions that help grow the net worth of the company. However this is achieved, efficiency is the key, and companies are willing to pay individuals handsomely if they can increase the company's productivity. At the end of the day, waste hurts everyone: the owners, the employees, and the stockholders.

The same philosophy should be applied to your household. If you are not efficient with your money, you will have higher loan payments, less savings, and fewer choices—as far as what you can provide for your children, and soon enough in what you can provide for yourself. More specifically, you may have to work more years, live in a smaller home, or have less money to spend. Therefore, I encourage you to think of yourself as a CFO researching ways to more efficiently pay for the major expense of educating your children that you (and your family business) are about to incur.

I refer to those who see the big picture as CFOs, and those who don't, or haven't yet, as non-CFOs. My goal by the end of this book is for you to become a CFO, if you are not one already.

Those of you with high-school-age children know how fast college has snuck up on you. Retirement will do the same in not many more years. That's why it's important to be proactive with your retirement planning, instead of being reactive or winging it. After all, if you were a shareholder of XYZ Corporation, how would you feel if you read in the *Wall Street Journal* that the CFO of this company was "just winging it"? Not good, eh? Well, the same principle applies to your money and your goals.

Non-CFOs compartmentalize expenses. They think, "We're going to buy a new car. Then we will go Hawaii. Then we will replace the windows in the house. Then we will educate the kids. And then . . ." Wait, back up! Educating your children will probably cost them more than all the other expenses put together.

As a CFO, you need to think more systematically and keep in mind that how you plan and pay for each expense is directly linked to what will remain in your pocket afterward, for you and your retirement. Making retirement planning a first step allows you to judge what else is financially feasible. It gives you a tool to evaluate colleges—with all their costs, aid history, and available scholarship money—and decide which are realistically feasible for your child to consider.

The CFOs approach this process keeping two goals in mind:
- To provide a great education for their children
- To be as efficient as possible with their hard-earned money

On the flip side, CFOs want to avoid the following:
- Closing doors of opportunity
- Bankrupting themselves and their children in pursuit of a college degree

From this perspective, your goal isn't to get your student admitted to the most prestigious college possible, but rather to help him or her get the best education possible considering your family's resources and opportunities. If, at the end of the day, you choose to send your child to the highest priced and most prestigious college, let this at least be a calculated decision after weighing all the options. Tragic is the family that doesn't plan well, has few options, commits to a high-priced college, and winds up struggling with large amounts of debt.

As a CFO, you will want to step back and ask yourself, what is the purpose of higher education?

Part of the college experience is nonacademic. Students broaden their social horizons by interacting with many different types of people from different parts of the world and with a wide array of beliefs and views. From a financial perspective, the purpose of higher education is to prepare students to become valuable assets to their respective communities and economies. It is, in fact, an investment in their future earning potentials. Research indicates that college graduates will earn approximately $1 million more over the course of their working lifetimes than non–college graduates. In a sense, the huge payments made to a college are really an investment (like buying rental property) rather than an expense (like buying a car). From this perspective you would expect the earnings from this investment to pay back the capital you invested.

If you buy a house and find yourself struggling to keep up with the mortgage, it is sensible to consider renting out a room to help make the payments. By the same token, it is reasonable to let your college student take on some of the responsibility and share your investment commitment in him or her.

There are many reasons that support this decision.

1. Research indicates that students who participate in the costs of their education take their educations more seriously and do better in school.

2. Your child's future earning potential has the ability to pay back a portion of the initial investment.

3. Some of the best loans available (for tax and interest rate purposes) are student loans.

4. Expecting your student to share some of the costs will greatly help you achieve your retirement goals.

If a student borrows $25,000 over the course of four years of college, the debt and the payments would be comparable to buying a new car. Can the student handle that? Is it fair to ask for that contribution from him or her?

Your basic attitude toward your child and your responsibility as a parent will probably be strongly influenced by your own experience as a child. I usually ask parents two basic questions.

1. What percentage of your education did you pay for?

2. What percentage of your child's education did you plan on paying for?

Whether you answer 100 percent or 25 percent to the first question, or if you didn't attend college, your answer to the second doesn't need to be the same as your answer to the first. Times have changed and so have costs. Asking your children to contribute to their education is not unreasonable. If they can help with even one year's expenses, it can mean a lot to improving the financial picture of your retirement.

I am certainly not recommending a universal strategy for every family, but I do think it is important to look at all the possibilities while you are asking yourself why you are sending your children to college. As your family's CFO, examine your resources and optimize efficiency. Lastly, remember that time flies; however old your children are today, be proactive and begin your planning now!

In the following chapters I describe the scenarios I have found to be most common and the strategies I have found to be most useful. I trust you will find in these pages a number of potent tools to help you be a more effective and efficient CFO for your family.

2

Key Steps to College Planning

While your children are in grade school and high school you have the option of sending them to a public school for free or paying for private schools. However, when it comes to a college education, even public schools cost money, while private and out-of-state public colleges can cost lots of money.

Before jumping into the search and application process, you should understand the obstacles you will face and how to more effectively prepare for these financial challenges.

I have identified at least seven key issues to consider in order to successfully apply and pay for college. Some require more effort by the students and some by their parents, but the more you invest in each of them, the better your outcome will be in terms of finding the right college at a reasonable price.

1. Standardized test preparation
2. Career planning
3. The college search
4. The big business of college
5. Consistently rising college costs
6. Financial aid forms
7. Finding good college financial planning information

1. Standardized Test Preparation

Other than a student's transcript, probably no factor is more heavily weighted in the admissions process than scores on standardized tests. Given that these scores hold such weight, and given the fact that students have only a few hours (and a few chances) to take these tests, being well prepared is vital.

NBA basketball all-star Allen Iverson is famous in the sports world for downplaying the importance of practice. Once interviewed after having missed his team's practice session, he was quoted as saying, "We're talking about practice, man. We're not even talking about the game." Hopefully, your student doesn't idolize Allen Iverson and apply the same attitude when it comes to the standardized tests, because when it comes to the SAT and ACTs, practice definitely pays off. These tests are intense, and they require both stamina and knowledge.

Also important is knowing how to best take the tests. This knowledge can include: understanding how to eliminate incorrect answers and make educated guesses and how to structure a good essay, knowing whether or not to leave questions unanswered, and realizing what the test preparers are looking for in different parts of the test. Having these and other skills can add hundreds of points to a student's final score.

"Hundreds of points," you say. Don't take my word for it. In fact, as I write this, the Peterson's SAT Test Preparation Package, found online at www.petersons.com, even offers a money-back guarantee for enrolled students if their test scores don't increase by 200 points. In addition to Peterson's, www.prepme.com boasts in big bold letters that their students increase their scores by an average of 305 points. Yes, a combination of information and improved test-taking skills can contribute to an increase of hundreds of points, with a large portion of this improvement coming from the practice itself and the added confidence that comes with such practice.

Recently, there has been controversy about the value of test scores, and some colleges have changed their policies, making the standardized test scores optional. More cynical commentators have suggested that this has been done to increase the number of applications to these schools. Increased numbers of applications means increased revenue through application fees, and with an increased applicant pool a college can appear more selective. Whatever the truth of that criticism, it is probably in the best interest of students who do score well to submit their scores, even when these tests are optional. Not only will increased scores elevate their chances of admission, but they might also unlock additional financial aid that could save your family thousands of dollars.

2. Career Planning

I realize that it is extremely difficult for a seventeen- or eighteen-year-old to know "what they want to be when they grow up." At this age, most have been exposed to very few real-world employment possibilities. However, almost every senior in high school has likes and dislikes—things they enjoy and activities they would rather avoid—and exploring these in more detail may point them toward professions that would suit them well.

All too often students go through their high school studies mechanically. They work to get good grades because they are expected to. But what if they studied because they wanted to, because they knew that it would help prepare them for a vocation they found exciting? While career planning at this age wouldn't be suitable for every student, many could benefit when they see how their schoolwork can help them become who they want to be.

Career planning can also help prevent a college decision disaster. What do you say to a student who, halfway through his sophomore year in a business program, announces that he would rather pursue a writing career? Do you tell him to stick it out and study business anyway or encourage him to transfer to a college with a strong writing program and thus basically start over from scratch?

While few students decide to transfer and start over, a growing number are taking five or six years to graduate. While for some this is because they can't get into required courses, for many more it results from changing their majors. They have to take a whole new set of required courses in order to graduate, which means additional units, additional years of attendance, and additional tuition payments.

In summary, career planning can produce some very powerful benefits.

- Students who are aware of subjects that align with their interests may be more motivated and focused.
- Students will be more aware of what to look for in a college and how to choose one that can fulfill their needs.
- Reducing the need to change majors or transfer to another college can save thousands of additional dollars on tuition.

I recommend two very useful websites: myroad.collegeboard. com and focuscareer.com. They both charge small fees to utilize their services, but you could wind up saving a significant amount of money. For slightly higher fees and more handholding, it might also make sense to hire a college consultant. Information about these services is available online from the Independent Educational Consultants Association (www.educationalconsulting.org).

3. The College Search

All too often students apply to colleges for the wrong reasons. They're attracted to a college because of the climate, or because it has a good football team, or maybe even because their boyfriend or girlfriend wants to go there. If a student is going to excel and acquire the education necessary for her future career, more important characteristics need to be evaluated.

A good search needs to begin with careful consideration of the courses and majors that each college offers, the makeup of the student body, the size of the institution, and geographic factors (for example, rural or urban, far from home or near).

There are some excellent college search tools available online. Both CollegeBoard (www.collegeboard.com) and CollegeToolkit (www.collegetoolkit.com) are free, while there is a small fee for Petersons (www.petersons.com). There are also a number of useful college guidebooks. I particularly recommend Fiske Guide to Colleges, which provides insight on characteristics ranging from average standardized test scores to student/teacher ratios to social and extracurricular activities. A first round of research will help students create a list of colleges that might be a good fit.

The next step is to visit each school in person. This is crucial. Every school provides beautiful glossy brochures with pictures of the most scenic areas of their campus, but these can't substitute for walking the grounds in person, talking to students, and taking in the atmosphere of a campus. On a personal note, I traveled with my family many miles to visit a few colleges that were out of state. Halfway through my tour at one of these (a school that was one of my favorites after reading through various guidebooks), I looked at my parents and told them I was ready to leave. At first, I felt disappointed because we had traveled so far, but soon afterward I felt a surge of relief. If I knew right then, after thirty minutes on campus, that I didn't want to be there (never mind attending for four years), then I had accomplished my mission.

Visiting schools gives families opportunities to meet with professors, coaches, and current students; conduct interviews; and talk with the financial aid department. If you are going to be seeking financial aid, it's probably helpful to sit down in person with someone in the aid department to find out what kind of assistance they have available. Because schools handle financial aid differently, knowing the procedures and possibilities at the schools you are considering will make you a better consumer.

If you cannot visit a campus in person, I recommend you spend time on each prospective college's website. Many schools provide virtual tours and even have video clips of current students and professors, which may give you some insights. You can also purchase video tours of campuses through websites like Collegiate Choice (www.CollegiateChoice.com) and theU.com (www.theU. com). However, I cannot stress enough that nothing will provide your student with more valuable insight about whether a college feels right than actually being physically on a college's campus. Such a gut feeling may not be scientific, but it is worth a lot.

Making an extra effort at this stage is important. If your student finds himself unhappy at a college, there is both an emotional and a financial cost. Dropping out is not anyone's goal in this process, not yours, not the student's, and not the college's. Transferring may be a viable option, but making sure credits will transfer and adapting to a new environment is also a challenge.

As your list of potential schools begins to take shape, it is vital to be practical as well. It is hard not to like what you read about

Harvard and what its campus has to offer, but if it isn't realistic, you will save time and money by eliminating it from your list. You can get a good feel for a student's chance of acceptance by utilizing the data at some of the online sites mentioned previously. Another resource that can provide helpful insight into a student's chance of acceptance is College Admissions Services, Inc. (www.go4college.com). Based on a student's qualifications, this service can estimate with a high degree of accuracy whether a student will be accepted to a select list of schools. There is, however, a small charge for each estimate. (Readers of this book can get a discount by entering the code: th1055.)

4. The Big Business of College

No matter how idealistic you may be about those ivy-covered walls, the fact is that college has become big business. This is simply a reality, and you need to factor it in if you want to be rational and efficient about your college planning.

Like any business, colleges want to bring in as much revenue as they can. Standing side-by-side with the colleges are lending companies that are equally interested in students attending college. They, too, want to bring in revenue and would like nothing more than to lend your family money. There are, in fact, loans available to both parents and students that allow you to borrow the full cost of college, no matter how expensive a school is.

While such loans can provide a student with the means to attend the school of her dreams, before being caught up in the enthusiasm of the moment it's wise to think about your and her ability to pay back that loan at a later date. Are you prepared to take on a debt that will remain with you for years, possibly stretching into retirement? Equally important, what kind of burden will your child carry after graduation?

If you are looking to avoid overwhelming amounts of debt and to get the best deal on college, you need to adopt the attitude that you are shopping. Just as when you buy a car, you need to figure out what is in your price range, ask about financing options, and perhaps even haggle over the numbers. While there are differences in the process, in both cases you are a consumer purchasing a product, and you want to get the most for your money.

Where college is concerned, your first step is to know what you are looking for. Do you want a school that specializes in engineering or in business? Or are you looking for a liberal arts college? You should spend time investigating the product. Just as you would check Consumer Reports to compare different makes and models of cars, you should look at the *U.S. News & World Report* ranking of colleges and consult Fiske Guide to Colleges to help you evaluate different aspects of schools. Find out the real costs and the availability of financial aid. And, finally, communicate with the colleges on your list to see what they can do to help you financially.

Strangely, many families don't ever consider whether they can realistically afford some of the schools their children apply to. Just because your seventeen-year-old daughter is in love with BMWs doesn't mean that you have to buy her one. And, just because she loves the idea of an Ivy League college doesn't mean you have to finance her attending one. If, like most people, your pocketbook is limited, then you need to begin thinking about college like a prudent consumer. Certainly there is status in sending your child to a "big name" college, but at what cost?

I want to emphasize that the title of this section is not simply "college is a business," but college is big business. Take a moment to absorb the fact that more than fifty colleges have endowments that exceed $1 billion. In addition, these colleges have hired the best investment managers available to grow their funds.

With this in mind, don't feel as though you are imposing on a college if you ask for a few thousand dollars in assistance, especially if it is from a school that has just made tens of millions from its investments. And remember, in addition to their investments, colleges are taking in money from tuition fees, application fees, sporting events, and, oh yeah, gifts from alumni. (Hold on, I think Wesleyan is on the phone.)

Why is it important to understand the big business that lies within the educational establishment? Because if you don't approach choosing a college as a consumer-buying decision, it will cost you more, and that more may be your retirement. You need to research how colleges handle financial aid. You need to learn the ins and outs of need-based, merit, and private scholarships. And you need to learn how to best represent yourself on paper, whether on a college application or a financial aid form. No big business will hand out money if it doesn't have to. It's up to you to find out what is possible and then get the cooperation of the college you choose.

5. Consistently Rising College Costs

Since the 1950s the cost of tuition has grown at about twice the general rate of inflation. There are several reasons for this phenomenon, but that doesn't make it any easier to bear.

First, colleges are in competition with one another for the best faculty. Highly regarded professors are the best advertisement for a college, bringing prestige and an increased number of applicants. As the parent of a student, this may be something you can brag about, but it comes at a cost.

Second, colleges are constantly renovating old facilities and creating new ones. Whether it is a new gymnasium, a library, or a laboratory, colleges seem to be always upgrading or enhancing their campuses, and the price tag for construction is stunning. For example, in my area, MIT just announced a $750 million project and Boston College just announced their $1.6 billion strategic investment plan in faculty, academic programs, and facilities. From a marketing standpoint, new, modern facilities allow a school to distinguish itself. Again, as a parent, being able to send your child to a state-of-the-art college probably appeals to you.

Third, like other businesses, colleges must invest in the latest technology to keep up, and these technologies have to be updated frequently. This certainly isn't a bad thing. You want the college to be cutting edge, but it does contribute to increased costs to parents.

The fourth factor applies to public schools; this is the decreasing amount of money the government earmarks for education. This translates into more money being required from students and their families. This trend has pushed the cost of attendance at state schools way up in recent years.

Finally, costs keep escalating in response to the simple economic principle of supply and demand. If people are willing to pay higher prices, businesses will continue to charge more. Currently, the demand for higher education allows colleges to raise their prices every year, and people are willing to pay (usually through borrowing) despite these increases. Whether families truly comprehend the financial commitment they are making is another story.

Is this fair? I suppose it is fair as determined by basic economics and the associated supply and demand curve. Until consumers start turning to less expensive options, colleges can, will, and probably should continue to charge their current rates. After all, if you were the president of a private college and you were currently charging $42,000 per year for students to attend, and you knew that you could charge $46,000 without it hurting your ability to attract new applicants, would you? Of course you would, and they do!

I personally believe, from my first-hand observations, that a major contributing factor to this skewed supply and demand curve is the lack of awareness and preparation going into the college selection process on the part of many families. Concerned solely with getting their son or daughter admitted somewhere, parents say to themselves that they will deal with the cost "no matter what it takes." Combining the fact that it is now the social norm for middle-class families to send their children to college because they can acquire loans to meet the costs, you end up with lots of uneducated, anxious consumers with checks in hand determined to buy no matter what the costs. This is a recipe for financial disaster, and, unfortunately, I see lots of families throwing up their hands, liquidating retirement accounts, tapping into large amounts of home equity, or having the child borrow massive amounts to make it work.

On the bright side, there are a couple of trends that may alter the supply and demand curve over the next decade, though this is only speculative. It is predicted that by around 2010 the supply of college-aged students will decline. When this happens, some colleges may need to adjust their costs to become more attractive. In fact, this is already occurring on a small scale through financial aid policies, but it may be amplified in the future.

Another trend that may change the supply and demand curve is the growth of online education. Online degrees offer students the ability to work and earn an income while also studying for a degree (making it more affordable), to minimize residential expenses (living at home rather than paying the on-campus fees), and to complete their coursework at their own pace. Many public and private institutions now have online learning options available, and this trend is sure to grow.

The supply and demand curve could also swing to the favor of consumers, if and when they stop blindly accepting the high costs and begin to actively seek colleges that are less expensive or that offer merit-based and need-based scholarships.

6. Financial Aid Forms

If you don't like doing your own taxes, you probably won't find the process of filling out financial aid forms pleasurable either. Nevertheless, if there is one area of college planning where I believe families most consistently cost themselves money, it is in how they deal with these forms. Here are the four most common mistakes.

Not Filling Out the Forms

Whether it is because they assume they will not qualify for any assistance, or because the forms are just too daunting, many families don't apply for financial aid. For example, according to www.collegeboard.com, in a recent year only 53 percent of the incoming full-time freshman at Boston College applied for need-based aid. If you don't fill out the financial aid forms you automatically disqualify yourselves from some useful college payment options such as tax-advantaged loans and work-study programs. More importantly, you may be forfeiting your right to review financial aid offers with colleges later on if an unexpected circumstance should occur, such as the loss of a job or major illness. By not filling out the forms, the message you are sending to the college is, I don't need or want your help. Not a very good message to send.

Submitting Forms Late

Financial aid is drawn from an existing pool of money. Once that pool is used up, you are out of luck. You want to be first in line.

Filling Out Forms Incorrectly

You need to be truthful when filling out the form, but you also need to know what they are asking for. A good example and common mistake is how parents fill out the Free Application for Federal Student Aid (FAFSA) financial aid form where it asks for the total value of investments.

Filling Out Forms Inadequately

Many families fail to realize that retirement account balances such as IRAs and 401(k)s should not be included in computing the balance and so put in a higher number than they should. The difference could easily be enough to disqualify you for need-based aid.

Understanding how financial aid is calculated allows you to better represent yourself on paper. The following chapters will provide you with legal and ethical ways to maximize your chances of getting financial aid.

7. Finding Good College Financial Planning Information

The first place most families look for information on financing college is their local high school on the financial aid night. Unfortunately, most parents come away with one or more of the following observations.

- The school held the session too late in the process, sometimes taking place in late fall of the student's senior year.

- The speakers told them about the process of applying for financial aid, but not how to improve their standing within the financial aid system.
- They didn't walk out knowing whether they qualified for aid, or for how much, or which schools would give it.
- Missing from the evening were discussions of cash flow, taxes, estate planning, or investment strategies that may save money.

Term to know ▶ *Free Application for Federal Student Aid*

Commonly abbreviated as FAFSA, this form is universally required by colleges from students seeking financial aid. The first time a family can submit this form is January 1 of a student's senior year in high school. It must be completed and submitted each year a family applies for financial aid. For more information visit the government website (www.fafsa.ed.gov).

Parents often look to a school's college guidance department for assistance. I would certainly recommend making use of this resource, but keep in mind that each guidance counselor may be working with hundreds of students. Moreover, guidance counselors are not Certified Financial Planners (CFPs) or Certified Public Accountants (CPAs). They can help you select colleges, seek out private scholarships, and compile application and financial aid forms, but you shouldn't ask them for advice on how to handle your stock options for college expenses. Even the best guidance counselors in the country would feel out of place telling a family to liquidate their IBM stock, refinance their home, or take a loan on a retirement plan in order to pay for college. Nor are they in a position to tell you the most efficient way to pay for college in your family's specific situation. So, utilize guidance counselors as much as you can, but don't rely on them for more than they are qualified to give.

I have also observed that parents rarely get a comprehensive plan for paying for college from the financial planners, investment managers, and accountants they rely on for financial advice. Each of these advisors has an area of expertise that may be useful, but rarely is one in a position—and I have noticed that rarely do they have the interest—to help you create an adequate plan to meet the huge total cost of college.

Finally, families often rely on the experience of their peers, and this can be the most dangerous mistake of all. Keep in mind that not only is everyone's situation different but financial aid is handled differently at different colleges and universities. That's why the most earnest advice can be hazardous and costly. Following are just a few variables that may affect how much a family will have to pay.

- A student's SAT/ACT scores
- A college's average SAT/ACT scores
- A college's history of financial aid packages
- A college's available merit scholarships
- A student's special talents
- The geographic location of a college
- The parent's adjusted gross income

- The parent's liquid cash and investments
- The parent's equity in real estate
- The student's gross income
- The student's investments
- The age of parents
- The number of children in a family
- The number of children attending college at the same time
- Parents' previous marriages
- Parents' business assets and income
- If there is early decision, early action, or regular admission
- The number of colleges a student applies to
- A student's extracurricular activities
- A student's grade point average
- The reputation of a student's high school
- A student's essay
- A student's recommendations
- Family legacies at specific college

And the list goes on. I think you get the point. Each family's situation is unique.

In summary, have your student contribute to the process of planning for college through test preparation, career planning, and selecting colleges. Remember that the best college for your student is the school where he will excel. Just because friends and family attended a school or it has prestige or a good football team, doesn't mean it is the right fit for her. Know that college is big business, and that it is in your best interest to be an educated consumer. Remember to ask yourself how much you can afford before blindly committing to borrowing more than you want to or can repay. Be sure to fill out the financial aid forms, fill them out early, and fill them out accurately. Finally, to become good consumers, seek out qualified guidance and advice. A small investment early in the process can save you a lot of money in the end.

3

Financial Aid 101

There are three basic types of financial aid: private scholarships, merit-based aid, and need-based aid. There are vast differences in how each is obtained and how much is available under each category. Before we look at actual techniques for obtaining aid and/or increasing the amount you qualify for, here is an overview of the three different types of available assistance.

Private Scholarships

Many organizations—local and national groups, associations, and corporations—award scholarships to students who meet particular requirements determined by those who founded the scholarships.

These requirements may involve academic achievement, leadership qualities, athletic abilities, or volunteer activities. There are also scholarships available to students who meet specific religious, ethnic, or geographic criteria.

The good news is that this money is absolutely free. Before you get too excited, however, keep in mind that obtaining these scholarships is hard work and competition for them can be fierce. Typically these awards attract the best of the best in each category. So even though you may have a motivated student, you can't depend on getting such scholarships.

There are more facts you should know about these scholarships.

Of the total amount of financial aid available to help your family pay for college, approximately 3 percent is, in fact, made up by private scholarships. Therefore, you may not want to spend 97 percent of your time trying to chase down 3 percent of the potential money.

Typically, these awards are made for the first year of college only, and they are usually a one-time award.

Many college financial aid departments see this money as an outside resource and will often reduce your financial aid package dollar-for-dollar by what you obtained through private scholarships. For example, if you are promised $20,000 in financial aid from a school and then receive a private scholarship for $5,000 from your local Rotary Club, the college may reduce their financial aid package to you by $5,000. I know, depressing.

Therefore, although private scholarships appear to be a great way to cut down on the expense of college, keep in mind both the amount of effort required and the potential financial aid repercussions. For those who do not expect to qualify for financial aid, these scholarships are still a good avenue. Your high school's guidance department has a list of scholarships that are dedicated to the local community. Because these are not always advertised, your student may have to be proactive and inquire about them.

Here are some helpful online resources.

- www.fastweb.com (free online scholarship search)
- www.collegeboard.com (free online scholarship search)
- www.scholarshipexperts.com (free online scholarship search)
- www.petersons.com (pay site with six-month membership fee)
- www.scholarshipcoach.com (scholarship reference site)

Merit-Based Aid

Many colleges set aside merit-based scholarships to attract students with standout qualities they highly desire, such as outstanding standardized test scores, athletic or artistic ability, high grades in challenging high school courses, among others. They give this money to students they think will add value to the campus in some way.

The two most common among these factors are athletics and test scores because students who excel in these areas add to a school's prestige. Successful athletic programs bring in money to colleges through ticket and merchandise sales, alumni contributions, and through an increased number of applications due to the school's higher visibility. On the academic side, the more selective a school appears, the more desirable it becomes, the more selective it can be, and the more easily it attracts highly qualified students.

Earlier, I referred to the *U.S. News & World Report* ranking of colleges as a key resource in any college search. The numerical ranking system used in this list scores colleges in a variety of categories, including acceptance rate (the lower the better) and SAT scores (the higher the better). The more selective the college and the higher the average SAT scores of its students, the higher will be its ranking. A higher ranking, of course, makes a school more marketable. With higher prestige may come increased application numbers and more leverage to charge a higher price. Supply and demand is at work once again.

Colleges have an additional motive to attract talented students: such students are more likely to have successful careers. Having noteworthy or famous alumni not only adds to the attractiveness of a school but also represents a pool of potential donors.

So what does all this mean to you? It means that if you have a student a college desires, then there is a good chance that college will be willing to award your student merit-based money. Here again, the Petersons website (www.petersons.com) can be useful because it allows you to do searches by kinds of aid available.

Term to know ▶ **"Safety" Schools and "Reach" Schools**

A "safety" school is a college that is likely to admit a student. A "reach" school is a more selective college, but one that your student finds attractive. When applying to colleges, most students will want to include both types on their list.

I suggest taking a look at Petersons, then creating a list of twenty schools and calling them directly to find out about available merit scholarships and the criteria they use to award them. This process may seem laborious, but keep in mind that we are talking about thousands of dollars in potential savings. From a business standpoint, I would say this will give you a pretty good yield per hour.

While doing this, keep in mind that a student is more likely to obtain a merit scholarship at a safety school, where he would be one of the better academically qualified applicants, rather than a reach school. It may turn out that money is offered at the least attractive school on the list, and that your student is also accepted at the school that seemed the greatest reach but without any aid incentive. Don't be surprised or disappointed if this happens; at least you have options.

While it may also be that a college on your list doesn't have established merit-based aid programs, you shouldn't let this stop you from exploring other options. If your student is highly desired by a college with a large endowment, the school might be willing to award an institutional grant or scholarship. This is another form of assistance, sometimes referred to as "tuition discounting." The bottom line is that if a school wants your student, then you have leverage, and the college may be willing to adjust its offer to gain your commitment. Chapter 6 further explores some of these possibilities.

Need-Based Aid

Whether your student has specific talents in any particular area is somewhat out of your control. However, your ability to obtain need-based aid is much easier to predict than merit or scholarship assistance because it is calculated based on financial aid formulas that don't judge a student's qualities. In addition, you may be able to adjust your financial profile.

Colleges determine a family's need based on a number of personal factors—income, assets, age of parents, and more—as well as the cost of college. The following chapter is concerned with the details of these calculations. However, to provide an overview, there are two types of need-based aid: gift aid and self-help aid. As it sounds, gift aid is money you do not have to pay back; it comes in the form of grants and scholarships. Self-help aid is provided to you through loans and work-study jobs.

While free money always sounds better, self-help aid can be a great option. Some wonderful loans are available through need-based aid. For example, there are federally subsidized Perkins and Stafford loans, where the government pays the interest while the student is in school. Any smart CFO would accept that loan, allow the money to accrue interest during the college years, and then pay it off after graduation. Therefore, although need-based loans are not as advantageous as grants and scholarships, they still can be a very useful resource.

Work-study also has great advantages. It gives a student the opportunity to work on campus, earn some money that is not taxed by the government, and build her resume at the same time. I want to inject here my own personal experience with work-study, which gave me an opportunity to experience a variety of activities on campus. I worked in a café, at the athletic center, in the East Asian Studies Center, and as a statistician for the women's soccer team. I enjoyed all these positions, was able to meet more people, and got to make some money as well.

Finally, keep in mind that you cannot take advantage of work-study or subsidized loans if you do not fill out the financial aid forms.

4

Calculating Financial Need

The three most important letters in the college planning alphabet are EFC, which stand for expected family contribution. This is the annual amount a college will want from your family before it will provide you with any need-based financial aid. A college takes this number and subtracts it from its total cost. If your EFC is less than the cost of the college, then the difference is your financial need, or, in other words, the amount of financial aid that you qualify for. It looks like this:

cost of attendance – EFC = financial need

The calculation to determine your family's EFC should be done for, or by, every family while a child is in high school, preferably before his or her senior year. Knowing whether you will or will not qualify for any need-based aid can take a lot of the uncertainty out of the college planning process. It will clarify exactly where you stand financially and allow you to see what is possible.

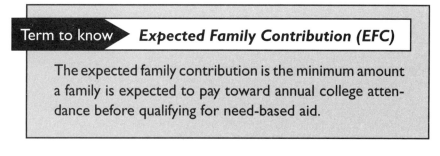

Term to know ▶ *Expected Family Contribution (EFC)*

The expected family contribution is the minimum amount a family is expected to pay toward annual college attendance before qualifying for need-based aid.

This calculation should also be performed on an annual basis once children are in college, since circumstances may change.

Key Features of Federal Methodology Used by Public Colleges

- Requires the completion of the FAFSA form
- Assesses student assets at 20 percent
- Assesses student income at 50 percent with a $3,000 allowance
- Assesses parent assets at 5.6 percent with an allowance typically between $20,000 and $60,000, depending on the age of parents (older parents receive a higher allowance)
- Assesses parent income between 22 and 47 percent
- Does not assess family-run and -occupied farms
- Does not assess net worth of family-owned and -controlled business with fewer than one hundred full-time employees
- Does not assess home equity

Chapter 5 explores ways to reduce your family's EFC so that your family may qualify for more financial aid. Implementing these strategies, however, requires an understanding of the two methods by which the EFC is computed. The first—predominantly used by public colleges—is called the federal methodology, while the second—predominantly used at private colleges—is called the institutional methodology.

The chart shows the primary characteristics of each formula.

Why are there two different formulas? The simple answer is that private colleges often have more money available for aid, especially gift aid, and they want additional information before giving it.

Key Features of Institutional Methodology
Used by Private Colleges

- Requires completion of the FAFSA, and, often, the CSS Financial Aid PROFILE forms distributed by the College Board
- Assesses student assets at 25 percent
- Assesses student income at 50 percent with no allowance, and assumes a minimum $1,550 contribution
- Assesses parent assets at 5 percent with an allowance between $16,000 and $30,000, based on the number of family members
- Considers assets held in a sibling's name as parents' assets
- Assesses parent income between 22 and 47 percent
- Assesses farm equity
- Assesses business equity
- Assesses home equity

For example, using the federal methodology, where parents' assets are assessed at 5.6 percent, for every $100,000 of assets they possess, their EFC is increased by $5,600 ($100,000 x 5.6% = $5,600).

In addition to these two methods, many private colleges have their own institutional formulas and/or may tweak the calculations to their own specifications. When looking at colleges, you should find out if they use the standard methodologies or have modified them. A second point to keep in mind is that asset-protection allowances do permit families to keep some money for expenses and emergencies that is not assessed in the EFC formulas. In general, the asset-protection allowance shelters somewhere between $20,000 and $60,000 of your money before it begins to get assessed. Older parents receive a larger allowance.

Several websites provide EFC calculators you may find useful, including FinAid (www.finaid.org), the College Board (www.collegeboard.com), College Toolkit (www.collegetoolkit.com), and SmartMoney (www.smartmoney.com).

Calculating Your EFC

Your EFC is derived from your family's financial profile using primarily four key factors.

1. Available Parental Income

Your available income is derived by taking your adjusted gross income (AGI) and subtracting certain variables, including paid child support and taxes (federal, state, local, and social security).

An income protection allowance draws the number down even further. This is intended to provide for the basic living expenses of all household members—more family members means a higher allowance. Finally, if both parents are employed, an employment allowance will further decrease the available parental income number. This allowance is 35 percent of the lower wage earner's salary up to a maximum deduction of $3,200.

Term to know ▶   *Adjusted Gross Income (AGI)*

Your AGI is derived from your federal income tax forms. This is your gross income minus certain deductions, including IRA contributions, the cost of self-employed health insurance, and alimony.

---

2. Available Parental Assets

Available assets include all cash and investment accounts (but not retirement plans), plus any equity in real estate. Home equity is typically counted by private colleges but not public. The formulas then subtract an asset protection allowance that is intended to accommodate the retirement and emergency needs of the family and factors in the age of the older parent—the older the parent the greater the allowance. The remaining value is multiplied by 12 percent. The remainder represents the available parental assets.

Your next step is to calculate the total parental contribution to the EFC, which is done by taking the total of steps one and two and multiplying by an assessment rate that varies from approximately 22 to 47 percent.

ALERT!

While the assessment rate is determined on a sliding scale, most families fall at the top end of 47 percent. The 5.6 percent figure for assets mentioned elsewhere in this book, and in most other resources, represents the total of the two calculations from which this number is derived (12 percent multiplied by 47 percent equals a 5.6 percent final assessment).

3. Available Student Income

Your available student income is derived by taking the student's total income, applying certain exclusions—including college work-study earnings—and deducting taxes (federal, state, local, and social security). After subtracting an income protection allowance of $3,000, the remainder is multiplied by an assessment rate of 50 percent.

4. Available Student Assets

The total amount of a student's assets is multiplied by a 20 percent assessment rate to calculate the available student asset amount. Adding available student income and asset figures produces your total student contribution.

Then, adding the total parental contribution to the total student contribution produces your EFC. The following example shows how these numbers play out.

5. The Freeman Family's EFC Calculation

Jordan and Jess Freeman, who are both fifty years old, are in the midst of helping their only child, Geoff, apply to colleges. Jordan and Jess have a joint adjusted gross income of $85,000 and possess roughly $75,000 in assets. Geoff earned $3,000 in the past year in after-school jobs. He has also managed to set aside $4,000 at his local bank in a savings account. In addition to this savings account, Geoff has $1,000 in Series EE Bonds, which were given to him by relatives as birthday presents. The Freemans are concerned with how they are going to pay for college and wonder if they can expect to receive any financial aid. Table 1 illustrates the Freemans' EFC calculation.

Using Your EFC to Evaluate Your Options

Knowing your EFC provides a powerful economic tool for evaluating your college choices. Let's take the Freemans' scenario one step further. Once again, keep in mind that every college handles its finances differently and that you need to be familiar with how each college handles need-based financial aid when you apply. By knowing what will be expected from you, and what each college will most likely offer, you can make some estimates about what you can reasonably expect to pay and what kind of help you will receive.

Table 1

Sample EFC Calculation Using FAFSA

Available parent income	
Adjusted gross income	$85,000
Federal tax paid	$9,000
FICA	$6,886
State and other tax allowance	$4,250
Income protection allowance	$23,070
Employment expense allowance	$3,200
Total available parental income	$38,594
Available parental assets	
Total assets	$75,000
Asset protection allowance	$48,700
Remaining asset value	$26,300
Remaining asset value at 12%	$3,156
Total available parental assets	$3,156
Total parental income + parental assets	$41,750
Total parental contribution at 47% assessment rate	$14,220
Available student income	
Adjusted gross income	$3,000
Income protection allowance	$3,000
Total available student income	0
Available student assets	
Total assets	$5,000
Total assets at 20% student assessment rate	$1,000
Total available student assets	$1,000
Total student income + student assets	$1,000
EFC (total parental contribution + total student contribution)	$15,220

The Freemans now know their EFC is approximately $15,220, but they aren't sure if this will cover their entire expenses or whether they can get further help to reduce this amount. Their son is hoping to study out of state and applies to several schools, including a public college, the University of New Hampshire (UNH), and a private school, Williams College. With UNH costing about $34,000, the expense is going to be a heavy burden, and with Williams at more than $45,000, it seems a pipe dream.

When the financial aid package arrived from UNH, the Freemans were devastated to see that although they showed a large financial need, they were offered a total of only $5,473 of gift aid toward meeting their financial need. In fact, the Freemans could have figured this in advance since the school's formulas are available online (www.collegeboard.com). Here's the formula the University of New Hampshire is reported to have used:

In-state cost	$21,609
Out-of-state cost	$33,759
Percent of need met	82%
Percent of gift aid	36%
Percent of self-help aid	64%

The costs listed above include tuition, room, board, books, supplies, and estimated personal expenses while the percentages are averages. With an EFC of $15,220, UNH recognizes that the family has a need of $18,539. However, the school is only prepared to help with 82 percent of that need ($15,202). It offers 36 percent in gift aid and provides the rest through some combination of loans and work-study student jobs.

Cost of Attendance	$33,759
Family's EFC	-$15,220
Need	$18,539
Percent of need met	x .82
Total financial aid	$15,202
Gift aid (36%)	$5,473
Self-help aid (64%)	$9,729
Family's contribution	$18,539

The bottom line for the Freeman family was that they would be paying $18,539 a year at UNH and would assume some portion of the $9,729 self-help aid in the form of debt.

The picture at Williams College, however, was even more surprising, but for different reasons. Here's the formula they use:

Private cost	$45,140
Percent of need met	100%
Gift aid	86%
Self-help aid	14%

While there is no advantage for in-state students or penalty for those out of state, the good news for the Freemans is that the school offers help for 100 percent of a student's financial need. After subtracting their $15,220 EFC from the total cost, this comes to $29,920. Even better, 86 percent is given in grants and scholarships, leaving only $4,189 to be made up in loans and work study.

The bottom line for the Freemans is that they will pay $15,220 a year and assume some portion of the $4,189 in loans. In this case it turns out that the more expensive private college will cost them less. (Note: Recently Williams and a handful of other private colleges announced that they will drop self-help aid from financial aid packages. Therefore, 100 percent of a family's needs will be met with grants and scholarships at these schools.)

Keep in mind that this is only a rough example. For the sake of simplicity, I haven't calculated the differences in EFC that might arise using the two different methodologies. It is a fact, however, that more gift aid is available at private institutions, so for those who qualify, the difference in cost between a public and private college may not be as great as it seems. Therefore, I want to encourage parents and their children to keep their options open by first calculating their EFC and then looking at the costs. Your family's net cost may not end up being the same as the intimidating advertised sticker price.

Cost of attendance	$45,140
Family's EFC	-$15,220
Need	$29,920
Gift aid (86%)	$25,731
Self-help aid (14%)	$4,189
Family's contribution	$15,220

Table 2
Sample EFC

Parents' AGI	Parents' Assets	Student's Assets	# Children in College	Public College Federal EFC Methodology	Private College Institutional EFC Methodology
$30,000	$0	$0	1	0	$3,517
$30,000	$0	$10,000	1	$2,000	$4,500
$30,000	$100,000	$0	1	$1,197	$6,886
$30,000	$100,000	$0	2	$880	$4,447
$50,000	$0	$0	1	$3,144	$8,030
$50,000	$0	$10,000	1	$5,144	$9,030
$50,000	$100,000	$0	1	$4,832	$13,617
$50,000	$100,000	$0	2	$2,851	$7,910
$75,000	$0	$0	1	$9,765	$16,478
$75,000	$0	$10,000	1	$11,765	$17,468
$75,000	$100,000	$0	1	$12,658	$22,118
$75,000	$100,000	$0	2	$6,931	$12,161
$100,000	$0	$0	1	$17,552	$24,265
$100,000	$0	$10,000	1	$19,552	$25,265
$100,000	$100,000	$0	1	$20,445	$29,905
$100,000	$100,000	$0	2	$10,824	$16,054

$125,000	$0	$0	1	$24,878	$31,591
$125,000	$0	$10,000	1	$26,878	$32,591
$125,000	$100,000	$0	1	$27,771	$37,231
$125,000	$100,000	$0	2	$14,487	$19,717
$150,000	$0	$0	1	$32,164	$38,877
$150,000	$0	$10,000	1	$34,164	$39,877
$150,000	$100,000	$0	1	$35,057	$44,517
$150,000	$100,000	$0	2	$18,130	$23,360
$175,000	$0	$0	1	$39,138	$45,851
$175,000	$0	$10,000	1	$41,138	$46,851
$175,000	$100,000	$0	1	$42,031	$51,491
$175,000	$100,000	$0	2	$21,617	$26,847
$200,000	$0	$0	1	$46,450	$53,164
$200,000	$0	$10,000	1	$48,450	$54,164
$200,000	$100,000	$0	1	$49,344	$58,804
$200,000	$100,000	$0	2	$25,273	$30,503
$300,000	$100,000	$0	2	$39,119	$44,349

The critical point is that when you know your EFC and how colleges award aid, you can plan for the cost and you can evaluate a bargain. Acting like a CFO and carefully scrutinizing the numbers of a potential purchase (in this case, a college education) gives you more choices.

Identifying Important EFC Variables

Examining the Freemans' calculations should help you understand how to do the same for yourself. At the same time, it's helpful to get a sense of how important variables interact. Table 2 shows how both federal and institutional methodologies treat family income, assets, and the number of children in college at the same time. Sample data is used, based on a family of four with the oldest parent aged fifty, home equity of $150,000, and no contributions to tax-deferred pension and savings plans.

Keep in mind that when these variables change, the numbers in the matrix will change as well. Nevertheless, examining the table can give you a sense of what you might expect. For example, line four shows that a family with an AGI of $30,000, with $100,000 in assets, and one child in college can expect to have an EFC of approximately $1,197 under the federal methodology and $6,886 under the institutional methodology. Scanning the numbers also reveals some interesting opportunities. Notice, for instance, how the EFC drops dramatically for students who don't have personal assets.

Planning for More than One Child in College at the Same Time

For those of you who are beginning to get nervous over college expenses because you know you will have two children in school at the same time, there is a small but significant silver lining. Looking at table 2, you can see that colleges dramatically discount your EFC for multiple students, which can make the difference in qualifying you for aid for each child.

For example, let's say that when your first child begins attending college your family's situation falls on line 15. You have $100,000 in AGI and $100,000 in assets. Your EFC by the federal methodology is $20,445. Then, two years later your second child enters college, so you have two in school at the same time. Now your situation falls on line 16 and your EFC is $10,824. This can make a huge difference. Those who didn't qualify when they were sending one child to college may now qualify for aid for both children. Those who qualified for aid for the first child will now qualify for considerably more for the first child and an equal amount for the second.

Interestingly, the biggest savings often come to those families whose EFC was initially around $50,000, and therefore above any college's cost. Such families usually assume that they will have to pay full tuition for all their children for all the years they attend college. However, when two children are in college at the same time, a great opportunity arises since the EFC for each child is now usually 50 to 60 percent of the original amount, or about

Table 3

How Your EFC Changes with
Two Children in College

One student in college and one student in high school			
Student 1 in college		Student 2 in high school	
Cost of private college	$45,000		
EFC	-$50,000		
Need-based aid	$0		

Two students in college			
Student 1 in college		Student 2 in college	
Cost of private college	$45,000	Cost of private college	$45,000
EFC	-$30,000	EFC	-$30,000
Need-based aid	$15,000	Need-based aid	$15,000

$30,000. If both attend colleges that cost around $45,000, each child now qualifies for $15,000 of financial aid. That equals $30,000 of financial aid each year that there are two children in college at the same time. And if they are two years apart with two years of overlap in college, this family is looking at perhaps $60,000 in potential aid. Table 3 illustrates just such a scenario.

In addition to illustrating a major opportunity for families with children close in age, this scenario also underscores three critical points made earlier in this book and repeated now because they are so important.

1. Don't wait until your child is a senior to calculate your EFC. You need to plan for opportunities such as this in advance.

2. Always submit a FAFSA form. In the above scenario, if you don't submit a FAFSA form for your first child because you know he or she will not qualify for aid, you may not be able to take advantage of the discount when the second child enters college.

3. Always contact prospective colleges directly. Ask how they assess assets and income, and which financial aid forms they require.

At this point, having seen the profound influence your EFC has on possible financial aid, you may also be asking the question that a good CFO would ask: "Is it possible to reduce my EFC, just as I reduce my taxes, by taking all the deductions allowed?" The answer is that there are a number of legal and ethical EFC reduction strategies available. Most families will find one or two that they can make use of. The next chapter examines these in detail.

5

Thirteen Strategies for Increasing Need-Based Aid

If you look carefully at the ways your EFC is calculated, you will notice that a family's income is weighted much more heavily than its assets. This means that a family with relatively high income and few assets is less likely to qualify for aid than a family with a small income but more assets.

Families with adjusted gross incomes above $150,000 or so will probably find more help in subsequent chapters, which outline strategies not related to need-based aid. A quick calculation on FinAid (www.finaid.org) using the following scenario shows why. A family of four with one student in college, the older parent fifty years old, $25,000 in savings, $150,000 in home equity, and an AGI of $150,000 yields an EFC of $37,000 by the federal methodology and $45,000 by the institutional methodology. Since these numbers probably equal or exceed the cost of attendance at the most expensive out-of-state public schools and private colleges, there is little hope that these families will qualify for need-based aid. However, remember two things. First, need-based aid is only one way to cut costs; and second, don't quit your job. A dollar in financial aid is not more valuable than a dollar of earned income.

Because this chapter is primarily concerned with strategies for controlling or changing the position of assets, those with more assets will find them more useful while those with few or none will find less help here. Also, keep in mind that what follows is a general discussion. Please consult with a personal financial advisor who knows your situation and a professional tax preparer before making any changes.

Strategy 1: Don't Hold Assets in Your Child's Name

The EFC formula assesses money in a student's name at the 20 percent rate for schools using the federal methodology and 25 percent using the institutional methodology. This means that every dollar your son or daughter has in a savings account will increase your family's EFC by twenty or twenty-five cents.

Let's assume that your son or daughter currently has $10,000 in a savings account, which was either given to them by a grandparent or accumulated from after-school and summer jobs. Unfortunately this carefully saved money would increase your family's EFC by at least $2,000. However, if that same $10,000 were in your account, it would only be assessed at 5.6 percent, thereby increasing your EFC by only $560. Simply by holding the cash in the student's name instead of your name means a loss of $1,440 of financial aid per year. Over four years of college, this could cost you $5,760.

Acting on this insight, if you can qualify for financial aid and are looking to increase your aid eligibility, you have three alternatives. One, you can have your children gift you their savings; they can gift $12,000 per person without having to file a gift tax return. Two, they can spend down their money on expenses that your family would have met with other funds. For example, they can buy a car for transportation, or a computer for school, or pay for application fees and other necessary expenses. And three, they can transfer assets out of an assessable account to a non-assessable account. (This option is discussed in strategy 2, below.)

Other common student assets are accounts set up for children under the provisions of the Uniform Transfer to Minors Act or the Uniform Gift to Minors Act. These accounts offer an easy way to give money and other assets to minor children while still maintaining some control over the investments. These accounts are taxed as the child's and, therefore, in most instances at a lower tax rate. While there may be a tax advantage to setting up one of these accounts, like a simple savings account they are heavily assessed when it comes to applying for financial aid.

Unfortunately, if you have set up one of these accounts, it cannot simply be terminated by pulling the money out and putting it in your name, as you could with a cash account. Legally, this money has to be spent on behalf of the child or given to him or her at age of majority (eighteen or twenty-one, depending on your state). Therefore, you are really left with only two strategies to diffuse this financial aid time bomb. You can spend this money on behalf of the student for necessary expenses, or have your child set up an UTMA/UGMA-owned 529 College Savings Plan. These plans are discussed on page 62.

In conclusion, the less money assessed at your student's rate, the lower your EFC will be.

Strategy 2: Don't Hold More Assessable Assets Than Necessary

Knowing how different types of assets are assessed in calculating your EFC allows you to make changes that can increase need-based aid. While every decision of this sort must be made within the context of your family's financial circumstances, you may have the potential to reduce the total out-of-pocket cost of college for your family by changing the nature of your investments and transferring assets into non-assessable accounts.

Remember that there are some important differences between most public and private colleges on a few items. Some private colleges require completion of the CSS Financial Aid PROFILE, which uses the institutional methodology and considers more assets assessable than the FAFSA.

 **CSS Financial Aid PROFILE**

The CSS Financial Aid PROFILE, which is administered by the College Scholarship Service (CSS), the financial aid division of the College Board, is used by many private colleges and universities to determine eligibility for nongovernment financial aid, such as an institution's own grants, loans, and scholarships.

In examining the two lists, you should begin to think about any assets you can move from the assessable side to the non-assessable side. Anything you can change will lower your EFC by the rates at which those assets are assessed. If, for example, you have $100,000 in cash, stocks, and mutual funds that you can transfer into non-assessable assets, you would reduce your EFC by approximately $5,600 a year, and, perhaps, qualify for $22,400 in need-based aid over four years.

Table 4, on the following page, shows which assets are assessable and which are not. These represent general guidelines, but keep in mind that individual schools differ.

Here are some opportunities to look for and issues to consider regarding specific categories of assets. Always remember to consider potential tax consequences and any transaction costs before making any changes.

Table 4

Assessable and Non-assessable Assets

Assessable Assets	Non-assessable assets
Cash accounts (checking, savings, certificates of deposit, money market funds)	401(k) retirement plans
Stocks	403(b) retirement plans
Bonds	457 retirement plans
Mutual funds	Traditional IRAs
Trusts	Roth IRAs
Coverdell savings accounts	SEP IRAs
UTMA/UGMA accounts	SIMPLE IRAs
529 savings plans	Keogh plans
Home equity (private colleges)	Annuities
Other real estate	Cash value life insurance
Business assets	Home equity (public colleges)

529 Savings Plans

Also known as qualified tuition plans, these tax-advantaged savings plans are authorized by Section 529 of the Internal Revenue Code and sponsored by states, state agencies, or educational institutions. In addition to their powerful tax advantages (discussed in chapter 9), they also offer a way to reduce your EFC; students who hold investments in UTMA or UGMA accounts should consider liquidating these and opening up their own 529 plans. A law enacted in 2006 prevents 529 plans from being assessed as a child's asset on the FAFSA. Private colleges may assess a student-owned 529 savings plan differently. Be sure to ask the financial aid departments at any potential college how it assesses such an asset.

ALERT!

Because 529 plans accept only cash into their accounts, if a UTMA or UGMA is in a stock or mutual fund, the investment must be sold before it can be transferred into a 529 plan, which will have tax consequences.

Home Equity

If your son or daughter will be applying to colleges that do not assess home equity, then it may make sense to pay down some home equity debt with assessable money. Not only will this reduce your EFC, but by reducing your mortgage payments you may improve your cash flow, which could be an aid in meeting college expenses.

Retirement Accounts

Your 401(k), 403(b) plan, or IRA should be one of your first considerations when looking to reposition assets. Not only is the money in these accounts non-assessable, but it also provides a tax deduction. And if, like most Americans, you have not set aside enough for retirement, making contributions to these accounts should be a priority anyway.

The only major restriction associated with moving assessable assets into retirement accounts are the contribution limits set by the IRS. The annual maximum amounts that one can currently contribute to these vehicles are:

- $15,500 for 401(k)s and 403(b)s or $20,500 for fifty or over
- $10,500 for SIMPLE IRAs or $13,000 for those fifty or over
- 25 percent of compensation up to $46,000 for SEP IRAs
- $5,000 for Roth IRAs or $6,000 for those fifty or over

For married couples with an AGI less than $156,000 or a single parent making less than $99,000, the first vehicle to fund in most circumstances is a Roth IRA. Money contributed to a Roth IRA is after-tax money, which means that you always have access to your contributions tax free and penalty free, though different rules apply to the interest or gains on your investment. Being able to access your contributions allows you to shelter money for financial aid purposes, but also keeps it available in case you need the funds to pay for college.

Take, for example, the situation where you place $5,000 in your Roth IRA and two years later you need it for educational expenses. If it's now worth $5,800, you can withdraw your initial $5,000 from the account tax free. In addition, the 10 percent early withdrawal penalty assessed on those who withdraw their earnings before age 59.5 is waived if the funds are used for qualified higher education expenses. More details on Roth IRAs are provided in chapter 9.

Annuities

If you have fully funded your retirement plans at work and Roth IRAs and you still have extra assessable money, consider funding an annuity. Because there are no limitations on the dollar amounts you can contribute to these accounts, this vehicle allows you to move very large sums of money from the assessable side of the EFC equation to the non-assessable side.

Less well understood than other retirement vehicles, an annuity is actually a contract between an investor and an insurance company. In return for your contributions to the account, the insurance company agrees to make periodic payments to you either immediately or at some time in the future. There are several different kinds of annuities and the choices can be confusing. They can offer tax advantages and guarantees as well as penalties for early withdrawal. If you are unfamiliar with the complexities of these instruments, it is advisable to consult a financial planner. Nevertheless, used properly, they can offer excellent benefits both as a retirement vehicle and for decreasing your family's EFC.

ALERT!

Although unusual, some private colleges count annuities and cash value life insurance as an assessable asset. Be sure to check with the colleges directly to find out their specific policy regarding these assets.

Trusts

Colleges assume that those who have trusts are wealthy, and, therefore, assess trust assets in their financial aid calculations. Moreover, there is usually very little opportunity to move trust assets into non-assessable assets. If you have a trust that places severe limitations on your access and the funds are unavailable to pay for college, then technically it really shouldn't be assessed. If this is your situation, I suggest contacting colleges directly to make your case.

Strategy 3: Don't Overestimate the Value of Your Home

The equity in your home is assessed when you apply to colleges that require the CSS/Financial Aid PROFILE form, or otherwise use the institutional methodology for calculating your EFC. Because it is one of your largest assets, you want to make sure you handle it correctly on the financial aid form.

To begin with, home equity means the value of your home minus liabilities against it. So, if your home is worth $500,000 and you have a $400,000 mortgage, then you only have $100,000 in equity. That $100,000 is used in computing your EFC.

Now, I know that you are proud of your home, but one of the biggest mistakes you can make is to overvalue it, and while the CSS form doesn't give a precise formula for valuation, it specifically instructs families not to use assessed, insured, or tax values. Instead, it asks for the price you could reasonably expect to receive for your home if you sold it today.

I suspect that, more often than not, parents put down a number that they would hope to sell their homes for. Moreover, when it comes to home prices, I have observed a strange psychology at work. People feel very comfortable being off by $20,000, or $50,000, or more, on the value of their home, perhaps because this amount represents a small percentage of the total value. Nevertheless, if you overestimate your home equity by $20,000, your financial aid will be reduced accordingly. I know it seems silly to lose aid because you guessed wrong on the value of your home, but it happens all the time.

To guard against either overvaluing your home or misrepresenting it as too low, I suggest using one or more of the online home value estimators, such as MLS.com, Zillow.com, RealEstateABC.com, or the Federal Housing Index Calculator at FinAid. org. I usually use the latter because it is also used by many financial aid departments to make sure people are not undervaluing their homes. The calculator uses two inputs—the year the home was purchased and the purchase price—and computes the current price based on tables used by the U.S. Department of Commerce. I have observed that the calculated figure is lower than the value assigned by families more than half the time.

In practical terms, if you estimate that your home is worth $500,000 and the calculator estimates it at $450,000, the $50,000 difference at a 5.6 percent assessment rate translates into $2,800 of lost aid per year. Over four years the overestimate would cost you $11,200.

At this point parents will often ask, "What if the college doesn't believe the value we put down?"

I offer three responses.

1. Most colleges use a financial calculator just as you have.

2. If, for whatever reason, a financial aid officer asks how
    you calculated your home value, you can say you ran an
    Internet valuation. This is probably at least as accurate as
    attempting to evaluate comparable homes through newspa-
    per listings.

3. I have never heard of a financial aid officer doing an
    assessment drive-by on a family's homes.

Finally, keep in mind that private colleges vary in how they assess
home equity in EFC calculations. Some may cap the amount at 2.5
times your household income. Others will figure in the full value,
while still others may not count it at all. Because private colleges
write their own rules, you should contact them directly to find out
how their formula works.

Strategy 4: Pay Off Debt

Sometimes parents ask me, "Will colleges take into account the
fact that I have $30,000 in credit card balances?" The answer is no,
they definitely will not. Therefore, if you have assessable assets, it
makes sense to pay off your credit cards. Not only do you reduce
your loan payments, which may carry interest rates anywhere
between 7 and 24 percent, but you reduce your EFC by 5.6 percent
of the assets you used.

In other words, if you had $30,000 in mutual funds and used
the proceeds to eliminate $30,000 of credit card balances, auto

loans, and personal loans, you will have effectively reduced your EFC by $1,680 (5.6 percent times $30,000). Over four years this difference could equal an EFC reduction of approximately $6,720. In addition, your cash flow should improve by whatever amount you were making in monthly payments.

Strategy 5: Make Needed Purchases

Another option that can work is to use investment funds to make major purchases before you fill out your first financial aid application. If you are going to put new windows in your home, fix a leaky roof, buy a new car or computer, then why not do so before you fill out your financial aid application, thereby reducing your assets and your EFC in the process.

Some people may laugh at the thought of spending money to reduce EFC. However, let me be clear. I am not advocating spending extra money but rather timing your expenses. If you are planning on making these purchases regardless of college payments, then moving them up can help you.

One issue that holds people back from liquidating their investments is the tax consequence. Keep in mind, however, that if these assets are earmarked for college, you are going to incur approximately the same tax consequences in the not-so-distant future anyway. So, feel free to liquidate your investments (after consulting with your tax advisor), and utilize these strategies if they make sense for you. Finally, try to liquidate any investments with gains before the end of the first semester in your student's sophomore year in high school. This will prevent the capital gains from showing up on your most recent tax return when you first apply for financial aid.

Strategy 6: Restructure Your Liabilities

Using investment funds to pay off your bad debt is one way to use your debt to advantage. It is also possible to turn bad debt, which only creates a drag on your finances, into good debt, which helps you reduce your assessable assets for financial aid purposes. In addition, this good debt may also be tax deductible.

The easiest and best way to accomplish this is by utilizing the equity in your home. There are two different ways to borrow from your home: a home equity loan and a home equity line of credit. With a home equity loan, you borrow a fixed amount all at once and then immediately begin repayment of the loan with interest. With a home equity line of credit, a specified amount of money becomes available to you based on the value of your home, and you can tap into it at any time. However, interest accrues only when you borrow this money, and you only owe interest on the amount you borrow, which might be far less than the amount you qualified for.

As a strategy to finance college, I recommend a line of credit as opposed to a home equity loan. A home equity loan forces you to take 100 percent of the balance you are borrowing and hold it somewhere until it is spent. Once you have possession of the funds, you need to put it somewhere, such as cash, bonds, or a conservative mutual fund, and suddenly 100 percent of this money is assessable in calculating your EFC. However, with a line of credit, you can access just enough to meet your obligations, so you don't hold extra assessable assets.

A major benefit of utilizing your home equity to consolidate and restructure other debts (personal loans, credit cards, auto loans) is that you will effectively be reducing the amount of equity in your home by applying these balances to it. Reducing the amount of equity in your home also reduces your EFC for private colleges, even though your net worth is still the same. Your assets and liabilities haven't changed in value, but by shifting your liabilities to assets that are considered for financial aid purposes, you have lowered your EFC.

For example, if you pay off your $25,000 in credit card debt with your home equity line of credit, you will have technically removed $25,000 from the value of your home. Since the credit card debt is not assessable and the equity in your home is, you have reduced your assessable assets by $25,000. At a 5.6 percent assessment rate, that could free up $1,400 in additional aid or $5,600 in aid over four years.

Besides potentially reducing your EFC by consolidating loans into your home equity line of credit, there are also other advantages.

- Low interest rates. Typically interest rates on loans associated with borrowing from your home will be some of the lowest rates you can obtain.

- Tax deductibility. Interest applied to your home equity will probably be tax deductible as opposed to interest on your credit card or auto loan.
- Simplification through consolidation. By having just one loan to pay off, your debts should be easier to manage. Simplification often provides greater control.

Though available to fewer people and, therefore, much less often utilized, margin loans on investment accounts can also be a source of "good debt." If you have an account of adequate size that is set up to enable margin borrowing, you can borrow on the equity within the account just as you would on the equity within your home. The benefit of this strategy is twofold. First, you can reduce the amount of assessable assets in an account. If you have a stock account worth approximately $80,000, and you take out a margin loan for $30,000 to pay off your credit cards, you only have to report $50,000 worth of value on the investment account, thus reducing your EFC. Second, you can access money in your accounts without being forced to liquidate your positions, thus avoiding a taxable event.

Strategy 7: Control Your Income

Most of the strategies in this chapter are linked to a family's assets. Unfortunately, the most influential factor in determining a family's EFC is the one you probably have the least control over: income. There are, however, a couple of instances where you may be able exercise some control.

If you have a high school senior, and you have some say over when and how you receive bonuses, commissions, or promotions at work, consider receiving the additional income the following year. This way you can report lower EFC numbers for your student's freshman year.

If you have stock options through your employer, or major positions in a few investments (maybe inherited), you should think carefully about your timing in liquidating these investments. There are a number of factors that need to be considered, including your EFC, taxes, the risks inherent in your investment portfolio, and how these assets fall into your overall college plan. In holding onto such assets, you know that they will be assessed as part of your EFC at the asset rate of 5.6 percent. If, however, you sell them, your gains will be assessed as income, perhaps at the 47 percent rate, so you need to do a breakeven analysis before making such a move. Moreover, if you liquidate a large investment in your student's senior year—and thereby, for example, double your annual income of $60,000 to $120,000—a financial aid officer may look at the income statement and be less sympathetic toward requests for subsequent years. This is another reason why planning for college expenses well in advance is so important.

Strategy 8: Carefully Time When You Sell Investments

The optimal way to liquidate investments when it comes to paying for college is the exact opposite of what seems intuitively true and what most parents believe.

It's safe to say that most people plan to pay for college by first utilizing their saved assets, then borrowing what they need at the end. As noted above, the problem with this scenario is that when you liquidate your investments, you increase your income, pay more taxes, raise your EFC, and reduce the amount of financial aid you qualify for.

If you have done some financial planning and know in advance that you are going to have to borrow a certain amount to pay for four years of college, consider borrowing a portion up front. If you borrow first and hold onto your investments, you give your investments more time to grow while avoiding the penalty associated with increased income.

Your first financial aid form can actually be completed on January 1 of your student's senior year in high school. Financial aid forms for each year your child is in college can also be completed on January 1. Your last financial aid form can be completed on January 1 of your student's junior year of college. This means that during his or her last three college semesters—the second semester of the junior year and all of the senior year—any additional income you may receive (by selling your investments for instance) will have no impact on financial aid. After you have filled out your final financial form in January of your student's junior year of college, you can liquidate your investments without any financial aid implications, assuming, of course, that you don't have another child who is a junior or senior in high school.

The final five strategies in this chapter specifically address circumstances specific to business owners. Unlike their salaried employee friends who have only their incomes assessed in the financial aid formulas, owners may have both their business income and their business assets assessed, depending on the school and the size of the business.

The good news for business owners is that business assets are assessed less heavily than investment assets. New to the 2007–2008 FAFSA form, if you have one hundred or fewer employees, you do not have to report your business assets. For the CSS/Financial Aid PROFILE, and for those with more than one hundred full-time employees, only 40 percent of the first $105,000 is subject to the EFC assessment. So, if you hold $100,000 in business assets, your assessment will be 5.6 percent of $40,000 (or an EFC increase of approximately $2,240).

Moreover, as a business owner, you already know that you have a certain amount of control over how profits, expenses, income, benefits, and taxes are distributed. This flexibility allows you to position yourself more effectively for financial aid by reducing your EFC. Here are some of the most common strategies you can utilize.

Strategy 9: Don't Overvalue Your Business

Just as with your home, you don't want to report a number that is higher than the actual value of your asset. The financial aid forms specifically ask for the net worth of your business. Unlike your home, this is not the estimated value of your business if you were to sell it. The net worth is calculated by adding cash on hand, receivables, machinery and equipment, property, and inventory, and then subtracting accounts payable, debts, and mortgages. The final total is the number you should report.

Strategy 10: Use the Federal Commercial Property Calculator

If you have any additional real estate in addition to your primary residence, and you operate those properties for income, you may be able to claim those assets as business assets. Financial aid officers may or may not agree with you in categorizing these properties as a business on the financial aid forms, but if they do, the assessed value is reduced by 60 percent. To make sure you are not overestimating the equity in your commercial real estate, use the Federal Commercial Property Multiplier at FinAid.org to get an objective valuation, then subtract the mortgage balance to get the net worth of your investment.

Strategy 11: Reduce Your Income

Most businesses have some elasticity concerning cash flow, which you can use to your advantage when applying for financial aid. One tactic is to lengthen your billing period, so that more receivables fall into the following year. A second is to accelerate your spending—within sensible limits, of course. If you are planning on any equipment purchases in the next year, for instance, you might consider making them sooner. Both these tactics will reduce your profits and income for the year in question.

Strategy 12: Employ Your Spouse

In the EFC formula there is a line item titled, "employment expense allowance," which allows you to deduct a portion of the lower-earning spouse's income from your EFC in families where both parents work. The federal methodology allows up to $3,300 in deductions (35 percent of the first $9,429), while the institutional methodology allows up to $3,970 (44 percent of the first $9,023). If only one parent works, however, there is no deduction.

For the owner of a small business this can be helpful. Take, for example, a family in which the father is self-employed and receives $75,000 as income. Throughout the year the mother helps with the family business but does not receive any wages directly. What if, instead of having the father taking in $75,000, he only receives $65,000 and the mother is compensated $10,000 per year?

This scenario offers several benefits. While the family's income remains the same, now both parents have earned income. They qualify for the maximum amount of the employment expense allowance, and they reduce their available income for the EFC. In addition, because of her earned income, the mother can contribute to a tax-deductible retirement plan, which reduces taxes and shelters assets. Applying this strategy, the family can save money in financial aid and taxes while increasing its retirement savings.

Strategy 13: Set Up and Contribute to Retirement Plans

Business owners have a number of retirement plans available to them, many of which accept large contributions. These include 401(k) plans (usually used by businesses with many employees), solo 401(k) plans and SEP IRAs (typically for one-person shops or husband-and-wife businesses), SIMPLE IRAs (for small businesses with a few employees), as well as both traditional and Roth IRAs.

These accounts are not assessed for EFC calculations, and they offer substantial tax benefits. If you are a business owner and have not already set up a retirement account, you should make every effort to implement this strategy before your student is ready to apply to college. It is wise, of course, to consult with a qualified financial advisor about which plan would be most appropriate for you.

6

Improving Your Aid Award Even More

Because every college is unique and has its own policies and rules regarding financial aid, you have to keep in mind that not every aid award will be the same or even equivalent. Once you have heard from the financial aid departments of the colleges where your student has been admitted, evaluate each financial aid package very carefully and ask yourself the following questions.

- Did they meet 100 percent of our need?
- How much gift aid did they award?
- How much self-help aid did they award?
- What types of loans did they include?
- How does our package compare to their typical package

(as reported by collegeboard.com)?

- If we receive private (outside) scholarships, how does that affect our package?

- Finally, what will our actual out-of-pocket expenses be?

With this information in hand, you can now ask the more difficult questions.

- How does our student compare academically to the college's average student?

- Which schools would provide a better college education? Which would provide the best?

- How does our student rank his desire to attend each institution?

- Which college can we realistically afford?

It's important that you and your student discuss these issues before moving forward.

How and When to Appeal the Aid Package

Once an offer for financial aid is on the table, there is one last chance for improving your package. Though some colleges will refuse to reconsider their aid packages, many colleges have in place a formal appeals process that allows financial aid officers to exercise their professional judgment and make adjustments. This is the power you hope they will exercise to your advantage.

You may have heard that you can "negotiate" with colleges on your aid package. I suggest that you avoid using this term, which is loathed by colleges, and avoid being confrontational. Remember that financial aid officers are human beings doing the jobs they were hired to do and treat them with respect. If you make demands and express hostility, I am guessing that you will be shown little sympathy. This is, I know, simple common sense. Still it needs to be repeated.

When do I believe you are justified in filing or requesting an appeal? I submit that you are almost always justified. College is a huge investment, and you have every right to try to reduce the burden for your sake and your student's.

That said, the real question is, when will a college feel you are justified? In general, there are three circumstances that will move a college to reconsider.

1. There was an error in calculating your family's EFC and/or the school has offered your family less than the standard package usually offered to those in your situation.

2. You have a special circumstance that was not taken into consideration.

3. Your student is highly desired by the college.

The first is rather self-evident, but I include it as a reminder that sometimes mistakes are made. If the numbers don't look right, don't accept them.

The second scenario might arise from a variety of circumstances that either do not show up on financial aid forms or that arose subsequently. These might include unusually high family medical expenses or child care costs, a one-year income spike that won't be repeated, recent unemployment, assets that raised your EFC but may not be accessible or liquid, younger siblings' education costs, and divorce or separation of parents. Any of these situations would warrant getting in touch with a college's financial aid officer to see if further help might be available.

The third scenario is the most complex and also represents the area where financial aid officers are likely to have some unadvertised prerogatives. If your student has a high academic ranking, a special talent, or would add geographic or cultural diversity to the incoming class, he or she may have something the school wants, and this gives you some leverage. (A detailed discussion of how to create and use this leverage appears on page 84).

Keep in mind that time is of the essence. The admissions process is stressful and time consuming for colleges. Schools want to lock in their freshman class as efficiently as possible, and a college's pool of financial aid money gets depleted as it admits students. Therefore, once you have received and evaluated offers, you need to act quickly if you are to appeal successfully.

First, find out if the college has a formal appeals process, and if they do, follow their guidelines. Then carefully gather your facts and either send a letter or make out an outline to use as a guide when you talk to someone, either on the phone or in person. The kind of comprehensive planning outlined in this book will be a major advantage at this point. If you know your numbers, and you know the college and its numbers, it will be much easier for you to plead your case.

Here is a sample letter appealing a financial aid offer.

Dear Financial Aid Officer, University of America,

I am writing to thank you for the financial aid package you have offered my son, Thomas, and to request that you consider amending the offer in the light of some additional information. Thank you for the assistance you have offered and for taking the time to allow us to follow up with you. I am sure you can appreciate what a major financial decision this is for our family. Currently, Thomas has been accepted by five other schools, three of which have made generous financial aid packages (letters attached). As the University of America is Thomas' number one choice, this has put us in a difficult bind. I hope you will consider some additional information (listed below), in hopes that you may use your professional judgment to see if there is anything else you can do to make attending University of America more financially feasible for Thomas.

• Mrs. Van Vleck has been ill and unable to work. This has put an additional strain on our cash flow.

• Thomas' younger brother, James, will be entering a private high school next year. This will increase our expenses by an additional $10,000 per year.

• Mr. Van Vleck's income was unusually high this past year because of a one-time bonus that was paid out to all Factory USA employees. We have been told not to expect any bonuses moving forward.

Again, University of America is his first choice, and if there is anything you can do to help us better manage your school's cost of attendance, it would be greatly appreciated.

Thank you for your time and consideration. Please feel free to call (555-123-1212) or email (Vleck@email.com) if you have any further questions or need any additional information from us.

Sincerely,

Mr. and Mrs. Van Vleck

Although your situation will not be the same as the Van Vlecks, your approach could be similar. Be courteous, explain your special circumstances, and ask for help. In addition, you should always express your student's genuine desire to attend the college, request that the aid officer use his or her professional judgment, and give specific reasons for the appeal.

After all, if you are cordial and respectful, the worst that can happen is that they will say no. Also, keep in mind that your appeal will probably not be heard unless you have put in the effort to fill out the financial aid forms properly in the first place.

Create Leverage by Increasing Competition

Although some may consider the analogy a little crass, applying to colleges is much like buying a car. For you, education is a major expense—maybe equivalent to a new car every year for four years—while the college, like the car dealer, wants to make the sale at the highest price it can with the least amount of work. Part of your leverage in either situation comes from shopping around and creating a sense of competition. If you reach the stage of appealing an aid award, your chance of getting a favorable response is higher when several colleges are competing for your student.

I recommend that students apply to at least six schools: two safety schools, two reach schools, and two midrange schools that represent a fairly good chance of acceptance. You may want to include in this list one in-state school so that you can be sure to have a lower offer in writing, and one out-of-state school because colleges are always trying to recruit a geographically diverse student body. It may also be helpful to apply to a pair of schools in the same athletic conference because colleges hate to lose their applicants to their rivals.

The online version of the FAFSA financial aid form contains ten spaces for colleges where you want your financial aid form sent. By entering in these colleges all your data will automatically be forwarded to them.

In addition, every college you list will see the names of the other colleges you have entered. Therefore, Dartmouth now knows that they are competing with Yale, Princeton, Boston College, and UMass for your student. Conversely, if your daughter has only applied to Dartmouth, the school knows they have no competition.

Imagine that you are the chief financial aid officer at a private college. You receive Joe Smith's application for financial aid and notice that only your school is listed on the FAFSA form. Joe Smith is an average student. He doesn't really stand out athletically or artistically, while his test scores and GPA are in the midrange you accept for admission. How anxious are you to have Joe Smith attend your school? If you don't offer him financial aid or offer him less than you can, what is he going to do? As the chief financial aid officer, your duty is to disperse the school's assets for maximum possible effect. Why would you hand extra dollars to someone who will most likely be willing to pay full price?

Now, to be fair, colleges do their best to award financial aid to those who qualify based on need. Will a college go beyond that? Probably not in this case.

This scenario is more common than you may think. Families often don't apply to enough colleges for a variety of reasons: application fees, laziness, or perhaps they are sold on one particular school. Whatever the reason may be, by limiting their options and leverage, these families may be in for a disappointment when they receive their aid award package.

Create Leverage by Developing Relationships on Campus

Colleges want students who want to be on their campus. When you demonstrate enthusiasm about a specific program, they are reassured that you will be a valuable member of their incoming class. Colleges want to avoid students who lock themselves in their rooms and talk on the phone, play video games, and, yes, even study 100 percent of the time. By showing that you will be an active member of their community, you are making yourself more desirable to the college.

If you want to study a specific subject, try to become acquainted with one or more of the professors in the department. Email them, write letters, or see if you can meet them in person during their office hours to talk briefly about their program. If you show interest in them and what they teach, they will be interested in you. You will win friends and create leverage.

For student athletes, I recommend writing letters to the coaches at all the schools being considered and setting up quick introductory meetings. They love it when athletes who are interested in their school and playing on their team approach them. It makes their job, which is in part recruiting, a whole lot easier.

Also, remember that colleges want to keep their professors and coaches happy. If a coach or professor wants a particular student, the financial aid department will look for ways to help that student attend.

Create Leverage by Avoiding Early Decision

An early decision program allows a student to apply to a college earlier in the admission cycle and be notified if he or she is accepted in advance of other students and other schools. These programs have gained in popularity because they give an extra edge to students who apply to very prestigious schools. Some statistics show that students who apply early have a higher likelihood of gaining admission. In addition, for those who are successful, it means that they reduce the stress of the whole college application process.

Nevertheless, there are some negative consequences of applying early decision. Because the process of early decision requires a binding commitment, you give up any leverage you might have had for getting a better financial aid package. You have said, in essence, that your student will attend and you will pay for his education, however much or little is offered by way of aid. In addition, your student may be committing herself to only one school before she has really had time to explore the alternatives. Certainly students are doing a lot of maturing during this period in their lives. It is sad when students find out they are unhappy with the college they chose in haste or for the wrong reasons.

Not too long ago I sat in on a full-day college planning workshop sponsored by one of the leading college prep organizations. One of the speakers was a financial aid representative from an elite private college in the New England area. During the course of her talk she was asked by a parent whether applying early can have a negative effect on the financial aid package.

Her reply went something like this. "Well, I will give you two answers. The first answer is what my college would say, and that is that it will not have any impact." Then, getting off her chair and standing up in front of the crowd, she said, "My own personal answer is that it could, in fact, have an impact."

I appreciated her candor, and she confirmed what I had suspected.

Why would there ever be a difference in financial aid packages depending on when you apply for admission? The simple answer is leverage. If you apply early, they know they have you. And if a college knows that you are willing to take less to go there, they can allocate more generous financial aid packages for students they are pursuing—the missing flute player for the marching band, the award-winning high school chemistry student, the goalie for the women's soccer team, or the student with perfect test scores.

Putting These Strategies to the Test: A Success Story

Though I have changed the family's name, this is a true story. I don't recount it here to suggest that you will get these kinds of results—I don't know if I will ever see results like this again—but to show that the process described in this book really does work.

The Hewitts approached me for guidance on paying for the college costs of their daughter, Julie, who was a senior in high school. Being close to retirement age and with this large expense just one year away, they wondered if there was anything I could do to help them. The parents were an intelligent and informed couple who had already run their EFC calculation before I had even met them. They wanted to make sure they didn't leave any stone unturned when it came to paying for college, but, given that their EFC was in the $60,000 range, they were not very confident that they would get much help from the colleges their daughter was applying to.

I suggested that a comprehensive college plan would provide them with guidance on retirement, investments, and efficient ways to pay for college, whether or not they would qualify for aid. They saw value in a wider planning process, and we began working together.

We explored various strategies to reduce their EFC, with a focus on reducing their assessable assets. Using some of the strategies described in chapter 5, we found that the Hewitts could push their EFC down to about $40,000. Given that their daughter was applying to some of the more expensive private colleges, this might qualify them for a few thousand dollars in need-based aid. It wasn't a lot in terms of the total cost, but at least they were in the ballpark to be considered for some assistance. So, with a nothing-to-lose attitude, the Hewitts followed through on the strategies we devised.

A factor that tipped the scales in their favor was that Julie was a high-caliber student with excellent grades, high standardized test scores, and a fine overall resume. To the surprise of everyone, the family was presented with some very generous packages. A highly rated state school offered around $5,000, small private college A around $9,000, small private college B around $9,000, and an elite university offered $18,000.

Stop for a moment and think again about this. The Hewitts were doubtful that they could obtain any financial aid. They asked for help, took action, followed some EFC reduction strategies, and four excellent colleges came back with larger financial aid offers than any one of us had hoped. Even if the best offer they received was from the state school, it still would have been a victory, translating into $20,000 of assistance over the course of Julie's college career. Instead, not only did the Hewitts get a better offer from another school, but they got three better offers, including an $18,000 package from one of the best colleges in the world.

When the elite university offer arrived, the Hewitts had been planning a visit to the state school. Knowing they had a lot of leverage, I suggested that Mr. Hewitt set up an appointment with the state school's financial aid office to see if they could help even more with its high costs.

I gave this advice with several facts in mind. First, Julie had not yet made up her mind about which school she preferred. Second, I understood that asking for additional help would be uncomfortable for the Hewitts, as it would for most people. Third, the state school had previously told another client that they did not accept financial aid appeals. Nevertheless, knowing that they had leverage because of the other offers, I didn't share this last piece of information with the Hewitts.

In fact, the state school told the Hewitts they had "room to move" and bumped up their financial aid offer to $9,000. Having experienced the appeal process and realizing that financial aid officers want to be helpful (especially to sought-after students), with new confidence the Hewitts then approached the other colleges.

A couple of weeks later we were looking at four new offers for financial aid: the state school at $9,000, small private college A at $12,000, small private college B at $19,000 (trumping all previous offers), and finally the elite university outbidding all of them by increasing their aid package to $31,000. This was an offer Julie and her family simply could not refuse.

While the Hewitts' experience is extraordinary, and your son or daughter may not have Julie's qualifications, the techniques they used are available to almost everyone. You need to put in some hard work, but keep in mind that college will be a major expense for your family. As the CFO of your family, you want to make this purchase as economical as possible.

7

Twelve Cost-Cutting Strategies for Every Family

The previous chapter focused on obtaining need-based financial aid as a way of saving money on college costs. This chapter examines cost-cutting strategies that you can implement regardless of whether or not you qualify for need-based aid. Some of these strategies address technical issues, such as tax credits, while others focus on simple, direct ways to cut costs. Nevertheless, each one of these strategies can have a real impact on a family's finances.

Strategy 1: Get College Credit through Exams

There are several programs now available that allow students to get college credit for basic classes by taking and passing tests. This means that motivated students can take thousands of dollars in fees off their total college bill for a small testing fee and some extra effort. Imagine, for instance, that your student gets credit for her entire freshman year of college. Whether you are paying for a local public college or private school, you have just reduced the bill by 25 percent.

These discounted credits are available to almost any student who has the desire to pursue them, but desire is the operative word here. This is something that has to be done by the student, and it takes motivation. As a financial advisor, and not a child psychologist, I can't tell you how to motivate your student to make this effort.

What I can suggest is that parents talk openly and directly with their children about costs associated with college. Explain how paying for college is both a huge investment and a large expense. By developing a financial plan, you can look at what you can afford and share that information. Keep in mind that most parents don't grasp the financial commitment required for college, and students even less so.

If you are expecting your children to pay for some portion of their college expenses through work or loans, they can immediately see that they will reduce their burden by getting exam credits.

Currently, there are four major programs that offer such opportunities. Because not every college accepts every program, you need to do some up-front research to see what will and will not translate into college credits at the schools your student is considering.

Advanced Placement (AP)

Although taking an Advanced Placement course through your local high school most definitely will help you prepare for an AP test, it is not required. Currently, more than 1,400 higher education institutions give credit for passing an AP test toward their curriculum requirements. Thirty-seven exams are given that cover twenty-two subject areas, and the fee for each exam is under $100. Of the four testing options discussed here, AP tests are the most widely accepted.

Not only can AP exams save you money on college, but they can also help a student gain admission. Admission officers like to see students who challenge themselves academically and taking AP courses is a prime example. AP courses and exams are a double play for college planning, helping a student get into college and also saving money. Additional information is available online at the College Board website (www.collegeboard.com).

College-Level Examination Program (CLEP)

The College-Level Examination Program (CLEP) is a self-study option for obtaining college credits. More than 2,900 colleges and universities award credit for satisfactory scores on CLEP exams.

These tests are ninety minutes long and are primarily multiple-choice questions. They are scored on a scale of twenty to eighty points with a passing score of fifty. More than thirty exams are available for well under $100. Additional information is available online at the College Board website (www.collegeboard.com).

DSST

A proprietary self-study option, DSST currently offers thirty-seven exams. More than 1,900 colleges and universities award credit for satisfactory DSST scores. A list of accepting colleges and more information is available at www.getcollegecredit.com.

International Baccalaureate (IB)

The International Baccalaureate Diploma Program is a two-year course of study designed for students aged sixteen to nineteen. The international focus and high academic standards give this program high status for admissions at many competitive colleges. In addition, many colleges will award a significant number of credits to students who pass the IB exams with scores above a specified level. Currently 493 schools in the United States offer this program. For more information, see the International Baccalaureate website (www.ibo.org).

Strategy 2: Go Local

A lot of students glamorize the idea of going away to college, the farther away the better. I am not here to refute some of the benefits, but I want to point out the financial cost, particularly when considering public universities. After looking at the numbers, you may think twice before selecting an out-of-state public university over your in-state option.

In my home state of Massachusetts a lot of high school seniors decide to study at out-of-state universities such as the University of New Hampshire (UNH) or the University of Vermont (UVM). Both of those colleges are excellent schools. However, they are a lot more expensive than our largest in-state option, the University of Massachusetts at Amherst (UMass). Here are current room, board, and tuition numbers for these three schools.

	UMass	UNH	UVM
In-State Tuition	$9,924	$10,980	$12,054
Out-of-State Tuition	$20,502	$24,030	$27,938
Room and Board	$8,052	$8,168	$8,024

Here are the costs of tuition, room, and board to attend these three different colleges for a student whose home state is Massachusetts.

	UMass	UNH	UVM
Annual	$17,976	$32,198	$35,962
Four-Year Totals	$71,904	$128,792	$143,848

Thus, if your son chooses to attend UNH over UMass, it will cost you an additional $56,888 over four years. If your daughter chooses to attend UVM over UMass, it will cost you an additional $71,944 (twice the cost). At this point you also might want to ask yourself what $71,944 of savings could mean to your retirement. That amount, compounded at 10 percent annually for fifteen years, would be an additional $300,528.

Is it worth twice as much to attend an out-of-state public university? Is it worth that much less in retirement savings? Do these out-of-state schools have much better programs, facilities, and opportunities that make choosing an out-of-state college worthwhile? I leave that decision to you, but before moving on, I want to introduce a few more possibilities.

Each of the universities listed above has a room-and-board cost of approximately $8,000. Over four years that equates to $32,000 in expenses. What if you considered a local option and your student lived at home? This may be an awkward suggestion for some, but it should be considered by those not on track to financing their own retirement.

Another money-saving option is attending community college for the first two years and then transferring to a four-year school for the final two years. Students graduate with a degree from the four-year institution but pay community college rates for the first two years. This may be one of the most effective cost-cutting strategies available. However, in order for this strategy to work, a student has to perform at a level that satisfies the four-year institutions' criteria. Therefore, whichever community college program you select, it has to be a place where your student will do well. In addition, your student's course selection must fulfill the four-year college's requirements.

As a final option, if you and your student agree that you don't want to go local, you may want to consider Canadian colleges. Many Canadian schools, such as McGill University, are highly respected and cost much less than many American private colleges.

Let me pose a question to you: would you rather have $5,000 in financial aid or save $10,000 in taxes?

I ask because most families think that the only way to get help in paying for college is through obtaining financial aid. However, if you had to choose between $5,000 in aid or $10,000 in tax savings, would you still want the aid? I know it sometimes doesn't seem so, but tax savings really do put money in your pocket. Moreover, I suggest that you pursue tax savings as aggressively as financial aid. Strategies three through six offer substantial opportunities courtesy of the tax code.

Strategy 3: Take the Hope and Lifetime Learning Tax Credits

To understand the true value of these federal tax credits you need to be clear on the difference between a tax credit and a tax deduction. A credit reduces your tax bill dollar for dollar, while a deduction only reduces your taxable income. So, if you are in the 28 percent tax bracket, for instance, a $1,000 deduction will reduce your taxes by $280. A $1,000 tax credit reduces your taxes by the full $1,000.

The tax credits discussed below take a portion of the money you spent on tuition and deduct it directly from your tax bill. If, for example, your tax bill would have been $20,000 and you qualify for $1,800 in Hope Scholarship tax credits, your bill gets reduced to $18,200. These credits are in essence another form of financial aid. The government has recently put these credits in place to help you more easily afford the high cost of college. Work with your accountant to maximize these opportunities.

Another crucial element in these credits is that they can be used either by parents or students. If you don't qualify for any aid because your income exceeds certain limits, but your student can prove that he provided more than 50 percent of his own support—by paying tuition, room, and board from his own funds—he is eligible to claim a credit on his tax return.

The Hope Scholarship Tax Credit

In the student's first two years of college, parents can claim the Hope Scholarship tax credit equal to 100 percent of the first $1,200 spent on tuition and fees and 50 percent of the second $1,200. This means you can take $1,800 in tax credits if tuition and fees is $2,400 or more. To qualify, the student must be a dependent and attending at least half time.

Furthermore, this credit can be claimed for more than one student. So, if you have two children in their first or second year of college, you may be able to claim two Hope Scholarship credits. There are, however, income limits for claiming this credit. Once your modified adjusted gross income hits a certain level, the amount you can claim is gradually reduced until it phases out altogether. You can claim this credit on IRS Form 8863.

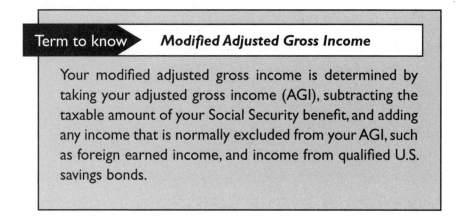

Term to know ▶ *Modified Adjusted Gross Income*

Your modified adjusted gross income is determined by taking your adjusted gross income (AGI), subtracting the taxable amount of your Social Security benefit, and adding any income that is normally excluded from your AGI, such as foreign earned income, and income from qualified U.S. savings bonds.

The Lifetime Learning Tax Credit

Another helping hand from the federal government, the lifetime learning tax credit is available throughout an individual's lifetime—not just the first two years of college—and allows you to take a 20 percent credit on up to $10,000 in educational expenses. You don't have to be a half-time student to claim this credit, but it is subject to the same income limitations as the Hope credit and can only be used for one person per family.

Strategy 4: Use Another Family Member's Lower Tax Bracket

Under current tax law, the long-term capital gains rate for individuals in the 10 and 15 percent income tax brackets is 0 percent for the years 2008 through 2010. This makes the gifting of appreciated assets held for more than one year a very effective tax-saving strategy. If you are currently in the 10 or 15 percent tax bracket, then you won't have to worry about paying long-term capital gains. However, if you are in the 25 percent tax bracket or above, any long-term capital gains you incur during these years will be taxed at the 15 percent rate. Therefore, a potential money-saving strategy is to gift these appreciated investments to someone who is in one of the lower brackets.

Here's a scenario to show how you can make this strategy work. Let's assume you and your spouse make a combined $80,000 a year and are, therefore, in the 25 percent tax bracket. Let's also assume that you own IBM stock worth $50,000, and that the stock was acquired fifteen years ago for $10,000. If you sell this stock, your long-term capital gains of $40,000 will be taxed at the 15 percent rate, meaning, you will owe Uncle Sam $6,000 in taxes.

Now, consider that grandma and grandpa, who are retired, are currently living on an annual income of $50,000, which places them in the 15 percent tax bracket. If the stock belonged to them, and they sold it instead of you, there would be no taxes due at all. You can, in fact, give them up to $12,000 a year without having to fill out a gift tax return. Therefore, if you plan ahead and gift this stock to your parents over the course of several years, no filing or taxes are due.

Grandma and grandpa can then sell the stock and use the money to pay for college expenses or, if you are receiving need-based aid, to pay off college-related loans after your student graduates. This is a bit convoluted, but the reason you don't want grandma and grandpa to pay tuition if you are receiving need-based aid is that the college will treat payments from other sources as they do a scholarship and may reduce your aid dollar for dollar. However, if you are not receiving need-based aid, grandma and grandpa can make the tuition payments for you. There is gift tax exclusion for payments made to cover tuition (though not for room and board or books), so there is no tax on these payments.

This same strategy may also work with your student, although it is more difficult. Uncle Sam has acted to prevent shifting investment income to children through provisions nicknamed the "kiddie tax." It states that all investment income generated above a certain threshold—currently $1,800—will be taxed at the parents' highest marginal tax rate. Therefore, following the previous example, if the parents gifted the IBM stock to the student to sell, all gains above $1,800 would be taxed at the parents' income tax rates, which would be worse than their own long-term capital gain rate of 15 percent. An exception to this rule is when the student has earned income from employment that provides over half of their support for the year. Therefore, if your student is employed and earns enough income to pay for more than half of her support, this strategy can be implemented.

Here's the scenario. Heather is attending her state university, which is costing $15,000 a year in tuition, room and board, and books. She earns $8,000 over the course of the year working part-time jobs. In this scenario, because she is providing over half of her support, her parents can gift her their appreciated investments, and she can sell them at her 0 percent long-term capital gains rate. This will also work for Heather after graduation when she is working and providing 100 percent of her own support, as long as she remains in the 15 percent income tax bracket.

Having considered their options in advance and developed a plan to pay for college as a CFO might, Heather's parents can gift her their appreciated investment after she graduates to help her pay down her student loans. Moreover, since she plans on being a teacher, she is unlikely to move into a higher tax bracket until the stock has been fully gifted and sold. In

ALERT!

Please consult with your tax professional before considering implementing this strategy. Also, keep an eye on the tax laws, which can change from year to year, since this strategy depends on tax rates and the treatment of capital gains.

this scenario, not only did Heather's parents get an additional four years of growth from their investment, they qualified for need-based aid, and they liquidated their investment in the most tax-efficient manner possible.

In this context, a word needs to be said about incentive stock options and nonqualified stock options. Similar gifting opportunities may be available once you have exercised these options, but be aware that if you qualify for need-based aid, improper handling of options can severely hurt your levels of assistance. If you exercise and cash out of options, your income may rise dramatically and, hence, eliminate or reduce your financial aid opportunities. If you don't qualify for need-based aid, this may be a strategy to consider. However, please consult your accountant or financial advisor and weigh all the elements in such a transaction, including portfolio risk, alternative minimum tax (AMT) potential, short-term versus long-term capital gains, stability of your stock, and any other elements that may be relevant to your personal situation.

Strategy 5: Employ Your Child

This strategy is for business owners and is relatively easy to implement. It provides tax savings to the family, helps build your child's resume, contributes to her work ethic, and puts extra money in her pocket. When you pay an employee, you deduct his pay as a business expense, so employing your child is beneficial to you by lowering the assessable assets of your business. In addition, assuming that the total pay is not a large amount, your student will not be heavily taxed on his earnings, if at all. Finally, since your student needs money for college anyway, this is a way to help him on a tax-deductible basis.

Suppose your student works for you every summer and earns $5,000 each year of college. Over four years this amounts to $20,000 of deductible wages to you and your business. If you are in the 25 percent tax bracket, your tax savings over this time is $5,000. Although $5,000 won't pay for their college education, I bet you would be pretty excited if your son or daughter came home with a $5,000 scholarship. Essentially this is the same thing—$5,000 gets to remain in your pocket. In addition, if you have more than one child, you can repeat this strategy and multiply the savings. As an additional benefit, any income that your child earns before college can be saved into a non-assessable and tax-favored retirement account such as a Roth IRA.

Looking at this strategy and the tax laws a little more deeply, you will notice that your child actually could earn a little over $20,000 annually without ever paying taxes on that income by the time their full standard deduction, personal exemption, and tax credits are applied. However, keep in mind that your student does have to do the work you pay them for, and you have to pay them a "reasonable" wage.

Again, I suggest that you consult a competent tax professional before you put this strategy into action.

Strategy 6: Establish a Section 127 Educational Assistance Plan

Another way in which a business owner may be able to save some additional tax dollars on college is by setting up an employer-paid tuition benefits program. Established by Section 127 of the Internal Revenue Code, this program allows an employer to provide up to $5,250 per year to employees, including employed children, as a benefit that is tax deductible to the business. Therefore, if you employ your child in your business, you can give her $5,250 each year she works to pay for school. The business is then able to deduct the benefit for tax purposes. This program can be used both for undergraduate and graduate school expenses.

Families that qualify for need-based aid should be aware that this benefit will reduce assistance dollar for dollar. Therefore, it is a more effective strategy for families that do not qualify for any assistance. Nevertheless, for families with a business, this strategy can help save money in taxes. A $5,250 tax deduction for those in the 25 percent tax bracket equates to a $1,313 savings each year. If you were going to give your child at least $5,250 for college anyway, why not make it tax deductible?

Strategy 7: Pursue Private Scholarships

As discussed earlier, if you qualify for need-based aid, private scholarships aren't the optimum use of your time, since in most cases the amount you receive will be offset by reduced aid. However, if you don't qualify for financial aid, then every scholarship dollar your student is able to procure will reduce your college expenses by just that much. The good news here is that those who work hardest at unlocking this money usually have the greatest success.

Think about the scholarship committee. Here are people reading dozens, maybe hundreds, of applications, often donating their time. They are going to be attracted to the student who has put a lot of time and effort into her application, come to their interview on time, dressed well, and showed her appreciation. Often a student's effort and desire for the scholarship can be transparently clear.

If you decide to pursue this route, I highly recommend acquiring a copy of *How to Go to College Almost for Free* by Ben Kaplan. There is a wealth of information on how to find scholarships, write your essay, and interview well.

Here are some other helpful resources.

- FastWeb (www.fastweb.com), free online scholarship search
- CollegeBoard (www.collegeboard.com), free scholarship search
- ScholarshipExperts (www.scholarshipexperts.com), a free scholarship search
- Petersons (www.petersons.com), $39 for six-month membership with a variety of services
- ScholarshipCoach (www.scholarshipcoach.com), a scholarship reference site with additional help
- Your high school guidance department

- Local businesses, including parents' employers
- State and federal governments

Strategy 8: Pursue Merit Scholarships

Merit-based scholarships are awarded directly by colleges. They are based on a student's outstanding achievements, test scores, or talents, and are awarded independent of need. There are three rules of thumb about merit scholarships.

1. Ivy League colleges do not award merit-based aid.

2. Private colleges offer more than public colleges.

3. Merit scholarships are mainly awarded to those at the top of an incoming college class, whatever the criteria, GPA, SAT scores, or athletics.

While there are limited resources for locating merit-based scholarships, I recommend the Petersons' website and *The A's and B's of Academic Scholarships: 100,000 Scholarships for Top Students* by Anna Leider. I also suggest contacting directly every school you are interested in.

A merit scholarship dilemma commonly occurs when students are admitted to their reach schools. Having achieved the best outcome they could have hoped given their academic record, just by getting in, their chances of receiving merit awards are low. If you find yourself in this situation, you may well ask yourself whether to send your student to the school she wants most, or to a school that is more affordable because it offers merit aid. It may not be an easy choice, but to have the choice is cause for celebration.

Strategy 9: Take Advantage of Employee Tuition Benefits

If you currently are employed at a college, your student probably qualifies for a significant discount on tuition at that school. I have, unfortunately, seen a lot of families simply dismiss this opportunity because students and their parents want to create the opportunity for separation.

Even so, if cost is an issue, I suggest reconsidering this decision. If your student is planning on pursuing a graduate degree, or if you have several children to educate, calculate what these savings could do for your own personal financial situation and for your retirement. You might consider having your student take two years with your college employer, then transfer to a different school.

Strategy 10: Guard Against Inflation by Prepaying Tuition

Both at private and public colleges tuition costs keep escalating at breathtaking rates, for many years averaging several percentage points above the general rate of inflation. This means that every year your student goes to college, the bill will increase, and, worse, it will probably increase more than your salary rises. Therefore, I encourage you to think big picture and see all four years as one prolonged expense. Table 5 shows how a 6 percent inflation rate on a $45,000-a-year college impacts your total cost over four years.

Table 5

College Tuition Adjusted for 6 Percent Inflation

Year 1	$45,000
Year 2	$47,700
Year 3	$50,562
Year 4	$53,596

If you think $45,000 is outrageous, wait till your student is a senior, when the cost may be $53,000 or more. Moreover, instead of paying the $180,000 over four years that you budgeted, the actual cost in this scenario will be $196,858. Is there anything you can do to make this burden lighter?

One possible strategy is to prepay for four years of college at the current cost. Doing this, you can save the $16,858 difference.

I suggest that you call colleges and find out if they accept prepayment for all four years. Many private schools do. If so, there are two vehicles that can help: an independent 529 prepaid tuition plan and the CollegeSure CD. Both are discussed in detail in chapter 9. The important feature of the independent 529 is that it combines the advantages of prepaying tuition and the features of a 529. This option can be utilized for many private colleges. The CollegeSure CD is an FDIC-insured certificate of deposit with an interest rate linked to the rising cost of higher education.

Strategy 11: Ease Your Cash Flow by Tapping into Home Equity

For many families, paying for college may be, more than anything else, a cash flow issue. They need to borrow money, and with borrowing comes payments. Unfortunately, an increase in expenses is rarely ever accompanied by greater household income. So how do you address this concern?

Perhaps the best solution, for those that will not qualify for need-based aid, is to utilize the full potential of your home. This disturbs a lot of parents because more than anything they want to pay off their home. This is the wisdom they have inherited from their parents, and the debt on their mortgage statements may be frightening. Nevertheless, families usually have more equity, leverage, and resources in their home than anywhere else.

For those who are hesitant to tap into their home equity to pay for college, a few questions may provide a different perspective.

- If you borrow from your home equity, does that mean your home stops appreciating in value?
- What will all the equity in your house ever do for you unless you borrow from it, take a reverse mortgage, or sell the home?
- If you do have to borrow for college, and you do not want to borrow from your home, what other loan offers such good interest rates, tax treatment, and flexibility of payment structure?

Depending on how your current mortgage is set up, you may be able to restructure it so that your cash flow will not be strained. Refinancing can, perhaps, extend the length of your mortgage, so you can pull equity out of your home and set it aside for college (possibly in one of the prepayment options mentioned above).

The potential benefits are many.

- When you pull money out of your home by refinancing your mortgage, you may be increasing your tax deductions. This means you are essentially paying for college on a tax-favored basis.

- If you extend the length of your loan, your monthly cash flow may be affected only slightly, thereby keeping your current finances consistent.

- You can save money by prepaying college expenses.

- You have peace of mind knowing you can pay for college.

- With college tuition costs taken care of, you can concentrate on one liability, your mortgage, which you may be able to pay down faster.

ALERT!

Consult with your financial planner and/or mortgage representative to evaluate mortgage options and consider different scenarios to evaluate whether these options make sense for you.

Strategy 12: Purchase Real Estate for Your Student's Housing

Another possible strategy for some parents is to purchase a small house or condo close to your student's campus. Instead of paying $8,000 to $10,000 a year for room and board for college housing or off-campus rent, you can apply that $32,000 to $40,000 you would have spent over four years to a short-term real estate investment. If there are additional rooms you can rent to other students, a good portion of your expenses might be covered. There is, of course, inherent risk in the real estate market, but on the positive side you could also realize some appreciation when you sell the property after your student's graduation.

Putting It All Together

Imagine combining some of these strategies. Before college you employ your children in your business and save thousands in taxes. Your student takes AP classes in high school and qualifies for college credit. They then save thousands more by aggressively pursuing private scholarships in conjunction with seeking out colleges that offer merit-based aid. You gift some appreciated investments to grandparents who sell them at their low long-term capital gains rate, saving money on taxes. You then prepay subsequent years of college either directly to the school or through a prepayment 529 plan and save the cost of inflation. And finally, for those with the resources and who have some understanding of real estate, you leverage room-and-board payments toward a property close to the campus, earning a profit on the appreciation.

Even if only a few of these strategies work for you, the savings can be substantial.

8

Special Family Situations

This chapter is divided into two sections, each addressing an individual family situation that can have a significant impact on college finances. The first section explores a variety of options that are available to grandparents who want to help meet the college expenses of their grandchildren. This section should be read by both parents and grandparents who are contemplating giving their grandchildren help with college. The second section describes how the EFC is calculated for students when their parents are divorced. It also offers some guidelines for optimizing a student's chances for financial aid depending on custodial arrangements and the relative financial situation of the parents.

Optimizing the Benefits of Grandparent Contributions

For those of you fortunate enough to have grandma and grandpa volunteer to chip in on college costs, it certainly takes a lot of the pressure off. However, before grandparents step forward to write a check, you should sit down with them and discuss different ways they can help out and the most advantageous strategies both in terms of tax advantages and your status regarding financial aid. As touched upon in the previous chapter, when you fill out the financial aid forms, grandma and grandpa's assets are not included in figuring your EFC. However, if they step forward to meet college expenses, colleges will suddenly look upon the money they provide as an additional outside resource. Just like private scholarships, any money grandparents pay directly to the school effectively reduces your aid.

Picture yourself, your spouse, grandma, and grandpa sitting on one side of a table as a team trying to finance your student's education. The college sits across from you on the other side.

The college says, "The cost for your child to attend our school is $30,000."

You say, "Oh no, after doing some financial planning we realized that the most we could pay is around $20,000 per year."

The college nods in agreement. "Yes, based on your financial aid application, we have come to the same conclusion. Our policy here is to provide you with a financial aid package that will make up the difference. Does that sound fair to you?"

You (greatly relieved), "That's great. We really appreciate that."

Just at this moment grandpa chimes in, "Well, grandma and I know that college is quite a financial commitment for you, and we would like to provide some help. We can contribute $10,000 a year."

You, "Thanks. You know you didn't have to do that, but it certainly takes some of the pressure off us. Thank you so much."

Grandma hands a $10,000 check to the college.

The college responds, "Terrific! Now with grandma and grandpa's help you can meet the full $30,000 on your own."

The college then withdraws its offer of financial aid.

I know this doesn't sound fair, but look upon it from a college's point of view. If you were the college and had a family qualify for a specific amount of assistance, and then the family gets thousands of dollars from another source, wouldn't you decide that this family is less needy than you originally thought? You would probably want to re-evaluate that family's aid package.

Thus, while the easiest way for a grandparent to help with college is by making a direct payment to the institution, this clearly is of the least benefit to families who qualify for financial aid. Instead, I recommend that you take advantage of as much financial aid as you can throughout the college years and do some borrowing to make up the difference. Then let grandma and grandpa pay down the debt after college.

For others who have done some financial planning and know that their family's EFC is high enough that financial aid is out of the picture, here are four options for grandparents that at least yield some tax savings.

Option 1: Pay the College Directly

Since aid is not an issue, payments made directly to the college will have no adverse financial aid effects; they will be exempt from gift tax, and they will also help the grandparents reduce their estate.

Option 2: Establish a 529 Plan

Introduced in chapter 5, and further discussed in chapter 9, a 529 qualified tuition plan is an excellent vehicle for grandparents who want to help with college expenses. Here are some of their many advantages.

- Money set aside grows tax-deferred.
- Money can be withdrawn tax free for qualified college expenses, so grandparents don't have to worry about paying additional taxes when they are liquidated.
- Money contributed to these plans is not subject to estate taxes.
- Grandparents can place large amounts into these vehicles at one time without triggering a gift tax: $60,000 for one grandparent, $120,000 for two grandparents. (This amount represents the $12,000 of annual allowable tax-free gifts multiplied by five. This five-year allowance is a special attribute of these plans.)

- Grandparents remain in control of the invested assets. They can change the makeup of the portfolio on an annual basis.

- Grandparents remain in control of who the money goes to and can change beneficiaries every year. If they would like to switch the account from grandson Robert to granddaughter Erica, they can do that.

- Finally, if need-based financial aid is a possibility, money held by a grandparent for the benefit of a grandchild is not counted as an asset for the EFC calculation, except in rare instances.

Option 3: Gift Appreciated Investments to Children or Grandchildren

This strategy is discussed in chapter 7 under the heading, "Use Another Family Member's Lower Tax Bracket." Here the scenario is reversed from the example given there. Instead of parents gifting assets to grandparents for liquidation at lower or no capital gains rates, the grandparents gift appreciated investments either to their own children or their grandchildren, depending on the circumstances.

In this situation, the grandparents might own stock that has tripled in value over many years; because they are in a high income-tax bracket, a significant amount of capital gains tax will be due when they sell the stock. If, however, their children are in the 10 or 15 percent tax bracket, the grandparents can gift the stock to their children, who can use the money to finance their children's educations, since the tax has been eliminated. In this way, they help with college expenses and avoid a significant tax bite.

Be aware that, once again, the guidelines enumerated in chapter 7 apply. Since this is a tax-saving strategy, timing, relative tax brackets, and special tax rules regarding gifts are critical factors.

ALERT!

The generation-skipping transfer tax (GSTT) may apply if grandparents gift the stock to a grandchild. Consult with your accountant or financial advisor for specific advice regarding your personal situation.

Option 4: Set Up a Charitable Remainder Trust

For grandparents who want to help their grandchildren with college and also include a charitable donation as part of their estate, a charitable remainder trust is a valuable tool. Here is an overview of how these trusts would work in such a circumstance.

The grandparents establish a charitable remainder trust and get a tax deduction for funding the trust. Typically, such a trust is funded with highly appreciated assets. The appreciated assets are then sold and converted into investment vehicles more appropriate for generating income. Because the trust has sold the appreciated assets rather than the grandparents, who were the original owners of the assets, there is no tax liability for the grandparents. The grandparents now receive income—a minimum of 5 percent annually—from the trust. This income can be used to help meet college expenses. At the death of the grandparents, the remaining assets in the trust are given to the chosen charity.

There are many benefits in utilizing this vehicle.

- Grandparents receive a tax deduction for their charitable gift.
- Grandparents avoid paying capital gains taxes on the appreciation of the asset that is gifted to the trust.
- The asset is removed from the grandparents' estate.
- The student gets help with college expenses.
- Whatever is left in the trust goes to the charity designated by the grandparents.

ALERT!

There are a number of different types of trusts that can be used to help grandchildren in addition to a charitable remainder trust. Please consult with your financial advisor, accountant, and attorney for more specifics and further possibilities.

Divorced or Separated Parents

Among the many financial complications involved in a divorce are the issues involved in financing college; these need to be considered when applying for financial aid.

Take the example of Betty and Bob and their daughter Rebecca. Betty, a yoga instructor, and Bob, a carpenter, each make $30,000 a year. During Rebecca's freshman year in high school, Betty and Bob get divorced. During Rebecca's junior year in high school, Betty remarries, to a plastic surgeon, Henry, who makes $400,000 per year.

Now Rebecca is in her senior year and sits down to fill out her college financial aid forms. In the style of her high school exams, here's the question: for her parents' income and assets, whose information should she enter?

A. Just Bob

B. Just Betty

C. Betty and Bob

D. Betty and Henry

Though not at all a trick question, the answer could be either A (just Bob) or D (Betty and Henry). It depends on whom Rebecca lived with for more than 50 percent of the time in the previous year, and this may not be the person who claimed Rebecca on their taxes. Here are the instructions from the FAFSA Financial Aid form:

> If your parents are divorced or separated, answer the questions about the parent you lived with more during the past 12 months. If you did not live with one parent more than the other, give answers about the parent who provided more financial support during the past 12 months, or during the most recent year that you actually received support from a parent. If this parent is remarried as of today, answer the questions

about that parent and the person to whom your
parent is married (your stepparent).

I purposely use this as an example because the answer is not intuitively obvious. In actual practice, many parents just guess because they don't know whose information is required on the forms, and they don't read the rules very carefully. Nevertheless, the wrong guess can cost them, or you, thousands of dollars.

Just compare answer A and answer D. If just Bob is responsible for filling out the financial aid forms, his $30,000 income would be used to calculate Rebecca's EFC. If Betty and Henry are responsible for filling out the financial aid forms, their $430,000 income is used to calculate Rebecca's EFC. Without even looking at the charts, it's obvious that in one scenario Rebecca will qualify for quite a bit of aid, while in the other she won't qualify for any.

If you are in a situation where there are dramatic differences in income between two separated parties, and it's possible to have the student spend more than 50 percent of their time living with the parent with a lower EFC, you may want to think through the financial implications where college is concerned.

On many occasions I have seen the parent with the higher household income take control of the financial aid process even though the student has spent less than 50 percent of his time with that parent. Here's a very common scenario. Joe and Anne separated when their son, Mark, was a freshman in high school. Since then Mark has spent about 60 percent of his time with Anne. It's now time to apply for financial aid, and Joe, who earns $90,000 a year to Anne's $25,000, fills out the financial aid form. By entering his own information in the application he violates the intent of the process and costs the family thousands in financial aid. This is a mistake you don't want to make.

Having said all this, I should add that some colleges have a supplemental form that asks the noncustodial parent for income and asset information. If or how a college will evaluate this information can vary and is difficult to predict. It's also possible that the college will consider further variables, such as agreements and stipulations that are part of a divorce decree. Other aspects of the parents' lives may come into play as well. What if Anne has a partner she lives with but hasn't married? What if a college asks for Joe's information but he refuses to cooperate?

If you are caught in one of these situations, I suggest communicating directly with a financial aid officer. Remember the first principle: the parent responsible for filling out the FAFSA form is the parent who took care of the child more than 50 percent of the time. After that, make sure you communicate to the aid officer any complicating circumstances that aren't described in the form.

The bottom line is that financial aid officers need to fully understand your situation so they can fairly assess how your student will be able to afford their institution.

9

Ten Ways to Save for College

I often have parents share with me tips their friends have given them regarding college planning. One of the most common but unsettling words of wisdom I have heard is, "Don't save for college."

I'm not quite sure what prompts that advice, but perhaps people think that by saving less they will qualify for more aid. Maybe they feel it's too difficult, or that whatever they save will be so little as to be insignificant. Whatever their motivation, I believe that those families who save, and save in the right places, have an easier time paying for college, no matter what their financial picture. Saving gives you options.

This chapter briefly illustrates why it's so important to commit to a regular savings plan and then discusses the various savings vehicles that are available.

Here are three hypothetical families in very different earning brackets, yet saving for college is important for each. Family one earns $30,000 a year. They will probably have a very low EFC and will qualify for need-based financial aid at most colleges. Even so, assuming that this lower-income family has very little discretionary income, any out-of-pocket college expenses will be a burden that most likely will have to be covered by student loans. It's unlikely that the parents will be able to borrow much, and they probably shouldn't. Thus, whatever this family can put aside to help their student get through college will be of great help.

Family two earns $100,000 a year and so are unlikely to qualify for need-based aid, except at the most expensive private colleges. Since this family has a lot more income than family one, the parents will probably be able to pay for a good portion of college expenses directly. Nevertheless, if this family has little or no savings, any remaining balance will have to be met by student and parent borrowing.

Finally, we have family three earning $300,000 a year. They will have a very high EFC and will have to meet 100 percent of college costs out of their own pockets. If this family has little or no savings, then all of the costs must be met by discretionary cash flow or through borrowing.

It doesn't matter which family you choose—if you give these families the option of tackling college expenses either with some savings or without, all three would say it's easier with savings. Having some money set aside gives a family flexibility and options, while a lack of savings in almost every case forces a family to take on debt.

Savings help everyone. The question isn't whether you should save, but where.

Any systematic savings program will help you toward future college expenses. It doesn't have to be much, but as you can see from the three graphs that follow, the earlier you start the better. The key is to start now at whatever level you can afford.

Table 6

Saving $100 a Month Earning 10 Percent Annually

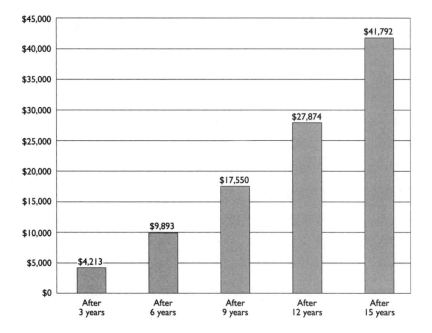

Table 7

Saving $250 a Month Earning 10 Percent Annually

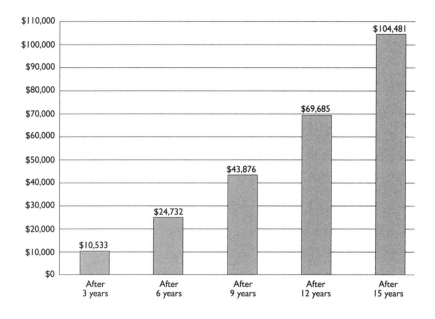

As these graphs indicate, the longer you put off setting up a systematic savings plan, the more dramatically the amount you will have to save monthly increases for you to reach your goal. For example, if your child will be heading off to college in fifteen years and your goal is to have $50,000 saved, you need to start today by putting aside $120 a month (assuming a rather liberal 10 percent annual earnings rate). If you put off this process for the next three years, you will then have to set aside $179 a month. If you delay for six years, you will need to set aside $285 a month, in nine years, $505 a month, and in twelve years, $1,187 a month. Table 8 provides a visual illustration of this point.

Table 8

Monthly Amount Needed to Save $50,000 in Fifteen Years

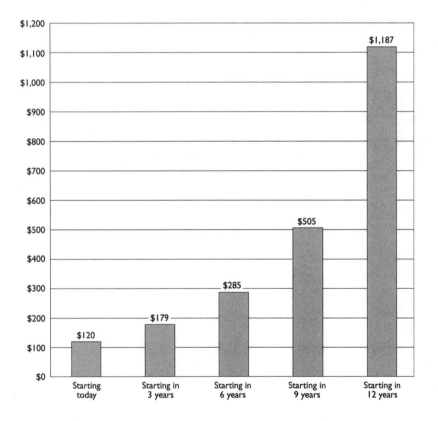

These figures suggest two obvious conclusions: one, saving helps; and two, you need to begin saving now.

The rest of this chapter examines ten different investment vehicles or programs you can use to save money. I describe the advantages and disadvantages of each and who they work best for. I also give each a report card with three grades: how it affects financial aid, how it is taxed, and the degree of control left in your hands. Notice that for the most part I don't discuss specific investments—such as stocks, bonds, mutual funds, or cash savings accounts—but rather the nature of the programs and vehicles themselves.

ALERT!

These are generic descriptions of vehicles and programs. Please consult with a qualified financial advisor about your particular needs and for more specific details about actual plans.

1. Roth IRAs

As discussed earlier, a Roth IRA is not only one of the best ways to save for retirement, but also has great advantages as a college savings vehicle. It is not assessed in computing your EFC, it grows tax-deferred, and your contributions are always accessible since they were made with after-tax dollars. Furthermore, the earnings in a Roth IRA can be withdrawn penalty free if used for a child's education.

At the risk of overstatement, this may be the single best savings vehicle available for qualifying individuals. When asked what one piece of advice he would give to families, a financial aid director in my area replied, "Everyone should have a Roth IRA."

Advantages of a Roth IRA

- Assets are non-assessable for financial aid.
- Growth is tax-deferred, and withdrawals at age 59.5 are potentially tax free.
- Owner chooses how contributions are invested.
- Contributions can be withdrawn penalty free and tax free.
- Earnings can be accessed penalty free if used for higher education purposes and account has been open for five years.
- Money not used for college can be kept in place for retirement.

Disadvantages of a Roth IRA

- This option is phased out for single taxpayers with an AGI greater than $99,000, or $156,000 for those filing joint tax returns.
- Contribution amounts are limited.
- Earnings distributed during college years will be counted as income on EFC calculations the following year.

Report Card for Roth IRA

Financial Aid: A

As noted in the "disadvantages" column, although Roth IRAs are not assessable for the EFC, distributions are assessed as income in subsequent financial aid calculations. However, if distributions are made after filing your last financial aid form—January 1 of your student's junior year—there are no negative consequences in terms of financial aid.

Taxes: A

Roth IRAs provide tax-deferred growth and potentially tax-free withdrawals.

Control: A

Owners can invest their savings in any way they choose. You can access contributions at any time penalty free and tax free.

2. State-Sponsored 529 College Savings Plans

Discussed earlier both in regard to need-based aid and as an excellent vehicle for grandparents, state-sponsored 529 college savings plans (not to be confused with independent 529 prepaid tuition plans) allow you to save large sums of money in mutual fund programs. Money placed within these vehicles grows tax deferred and the earnings can be withdrawn tax free if the proceeds are used for the beneficiary's qualified education expenses.

Until 2006, a major disadvantage of these plans was that money withdrawn and used to pay for college expenses could potentially be considered income in the following year's EFC calculations. Worse, it was figured at the student's 50 percent income rate, thus dramatically reducing the amount of financial aid that a student might qualify for. Federal law has changed the standard policy where FAFSA is concerned, and distributions no longer count as income. Nevertheless, private colleges can write their own financial aid rules. So, it is imperative that you research the rules at any colleges you may be considering and see how they handle 529 distributions.

Because the most significant benefit is their ability to grow tax free, they won't produce much in the way of savings if you have only a few years until college begins. Moreover, the tax-free earnings may be more than offset by the liability of holding this money as an assessable asset for the purpose of your EFC calculation. The following scenarios illustrate this point.

Scenario A: Money Placed in a 529 Plan Two Years before College

Here you are, two years before your child goes to college, and you have $5,000 to invest. Because you have only two years before you will need the money, you invest conservatively and earn, perhaps, a 5 percent rate of return. Your earnings would look like this. At the end of year one, your $5,000 has increased to $5,250 ($5,000 x 1.05 = $5,250). At the end of year two it is worth $5,513 ($5,250 x 1.05 = $5,513).

Now your family applies for financial aid and the $5,513 is assessed as an asset at a 5.6 percent rate, meaning that your EFC will increase by $309 based on the value of your 529 plan savings. You then withdraw your funds from the 529 plan to pay for college and enjoy the fact that $513 of the earnings is tax free, meaning that you saved $77 in capital gains tax ($513 multiplied by the 15 percent long-term capital gains rate). Nevertheless, though you saved $77 in taxes, having the money in an assessable 529 plan may have lost you $309 in financial aid.

Scenario B: Money Placed in a 529 Plan Fifteen Years before College

What if, instead of two years, you have fifteen years before your child goes off to college? With that much more time, you could invest your $5,000 a little more aggressively and earn, perhaps, 8 percent a year. Fifteen years later, with all your earnings reinvested and compounded, your account is worth $15,861.

Once again, your family applies for financial aid. Now your 529 plan is assessed at $888 ($15,861 x 5.6 percent). However, when you withdraw your $15,861, you are pulling out $10,861 in earnings and saving $1,629 in capital gains taxes ($10,861 x 15 percent). In this scenario, the amount you save in taxes is almost double the amount you lose in financial aid.

For those families who are thinking of college well ahead and know they won't qualify for financial aid, a 529 savings plan makes even more sense. They get the tax savings and lose nothing. However, if you only have a few years before college expenses will kick in, you may want to weigh the benefits of such a plan.

Be Aware of Tax Consequences

By now it must be obvious that successful college financial planning requires educating yourself about all the tools at your disposal and then thinking ahead to maximize your returns. Here's a scenario that illustrates these points as well as the pitfalls that await the unwary.

Sean is attending his state university at a cost of $15,000. Sean's parents invested in a 529 savings plan a few years ago, and with some good fortune their $5,000 investment is now worth $10,000. Sean is also grateful to be awarded a $5,000 scholarship from his local chamber of commerce. With both sources of money in hand, his parents are able to cover his expenses. Being savvy, they also know that they qualify for the lifetime learning tax credit discussed in chapter 7. They can receive the maximum $2,000 credit (20 percent of $10,000 in qualified expenses) deducted from their taxes.

However, the IRS doesn't allow families to double-dip on tax breaks. College expenses covered by untaxed student scholarships or expenses claimed toward the lifetime learning credit can't be the same expenses earmarked for 529 plan funds.

In Sean's situation, his scholarship covers $5,000 of the $15,000 in college costs, and the lifetime learning credit can be applied to the remaining $10,000. But this means that there is no balance to apply the 529 funds to. If Sean's parents liquidate the account and use the money to pay their $10,000 out-of-pocket costs, all the earnings will be taxable, thus eliminating the main advantage of the 529 plan.

ALERT!

Work with a competent advisor to plan exit strategies from any 529 savings plan accounts you hold.

In conclusion, while 529 savings plans are extremely popular and are one of the best choices available, I believe for many families they should not be the first and only place they save into. They work very well for families in high tax brackets who also have time to let an account grow. For families in lower tax brackets who will seek need-based financial aid and who have a relatively short time to save, they may be less effective than some of the other vehicles discussed in this chapter.

Advantages of a 529 plan
- Growth is tax deferred and withdrawals are tax free.
- Tax deductions for contributions are allowed in some states.
- Beneficiary on the account may be changed once a year.
- There are no income limitations.
- Each account has a high contribution ceiling.
- Plans from each state are available for investment regardless of your home state.

Disadvantages of a 529 plan
- Asset is assessable for financial aid.
- A 10-percent penalty is levied on earnings if not used for qualified higher education expenses.

- Many existing plans have high fees.

- Mutual fund options are limited.

- Investments may be reallocated once per year.

- Earnings are taxable if allocated to the same expenses as lifetime learning or Hope tax credits.

Report Card for 529 Plan

Financial Aid: A-

Money in a state-sponsored 529 college savings plan is assessed at the 5.6 percent assessment rate in calculating your EFC.

Taxes: A

Tax-deferred and tax-free withdrawals can produce significant savings. In addition, about half the states have programs that allow for state tax deductions as well. Further details can be found at www.savingforcollege.com for details.

Control: B

Unlike an IRA or taxable account, investment choices for 529 savings plans are limited. Changes to plans and/or beneficiaries are allowed only once a year. If you have money left over in a 529 plan—for instance, your child gets a lot of merit and/or need-based financial aid—there may be a 10-percent penalty assessed against those funds not used for qualified educational expenses.

3. Independent 529 Prepaid Tuition Plans

The independent 529 plan is a college-sponsored, national, pre-paid 529 plan that allows you to lock in future tuition costs at today's prices. This could represent a significant savings since college tuition has been growing at about 6 percent a year in recent years. In addition, participating colleges actually offer discounts of at least 0.5 percent off the current tuition. Because contribution limits are quite high, about $165,000 per account, it is possible to lock in four years of tuition at the most expensive colleges. At present only 260 schools participate in the independent 529 prepaid tuition program. So, if your student accepts admission at a college that is not one of the 260 participating schools, you lose the primary benefits of this account—the locking in of tuition rates. This plan works best for families in high income tax brackets that are investment risk adverse. Most important, your student needs to be quite sure he or she will attend one of the participating colleges.

Further details are available online at the independent 529 plan website (www.independent529plan.org).

Advantages of an independent 529 plan
- Earnings are tax free.
- Beneficiary on the account may be changed once a year.
- There are no income limitations.
- Contribution ceiling is high.
- Investment risk is assumed by colleges.
- Plans have low fees.

Disadvantages of an independent 529 plan

- Asset is assessable for financial aid.
- Plan is available for use at a limited number of colleges.
- Investment yield potential is limited.
- If used for a nonparticipating school, earnings are adjusted in relation to net performance of the program trust and subject to a maximum increase.
- A 10-percent penalty is levied on interest if funds are not used for qualified higher education expenses.
- Distributions used for the same qualified education expenses as for a lifetime learning or Hope scholarship tax credit are taxable.

Report Card for Independent 529 Plan

Financial Aid: A-

Funds in an independent 529 prepaid tuition plan are assessed at 5.6 percent in EFC calculations.

Taxes: A

Earnings are income-tax exempt.

Control: C-

Rate of return is determined by the college inflation index, and, more importantly, funds lock in current tuition rates only at the 260 participating colleges. This could potentially limit your control of college choice.

4. CollegeSure CDs

Issued by College Savings Bank, this FDIC-insured certificate of deposit (CD) pays an annual percentage yield indexed to the rise in college costs as measured by the Independent College 500 Index. This vehicle is designed for families who have a conservative risk tolerance and are satisfied if their investments keep pace with inflating tuition rates. Unlike the independent 529 plan, this investment is not restricted by choice of school. Be aware, however, that it does assess early withdrawal penalties. More information is available online at the College Savings Bank (www. collegesavings.com).

Advantages of a CollegeSure CD

- It is FDIC insured.
- It is very low risk.
- It keeps pace with college inflation.

Disadvantages of a CollegeSure CD

- A 5 to 10 percent penalty is levied for early withdrawals.
- Asset is assessable for financial aid.
- Account is fully taxable unless held in a 529 Saving Plan, Coverdell, or IRA.
- Investment upside potential is limited.

5. Coverdell Education Savings Accounts

Originally introduced as the Education IRA, the program was renamed when Congress expanded its benefits. Under the new provisions families may contribute up to $2,000 a year into a

Report Card for CollegeSure CDs

Financial Aid: A-

Considered an asset of the account owner for EFC calculations, the CollegeSure CD will in most cases be assessed at
the 5.6 percent rate.

Taxes: B/A

As with any bank CD, interest is fully taxable. However,
taxes can be avoided if purchased in a tax-favored account.
The CollegeSure CD is an investment option of the Mon-
tana and Arizona state-sponsored 529 savings plans. It can
also be used as a vehicle by traditional IRA, Roth IRA, and
Coverdell accounts.

Control: C

CDs have a limited upside earning potential and incur high
penalties for early withdrawal.

Coverdell Education Savings Account in either the parents' or the
student's names. The money may be invested in any way the owner
chooses—as opposed to 529 plans—and earnings accumulate tax
free. Funds can then be withdrawn tax free if they are used for
qualified education expenses. A unique feature of this program
is that funds may be used to cover qualified expenses from kin-
dergarten through senior year of high school, including private
school tuition, certain computer equipment and software, as well
as Internet access.

These plans are probably most useful to parents who will be paying for private high school. Lower income families should certainly make the maximum contributions allowable to their Roth IRAs before making use of this program and should keep in mind that they are assessable for EFC calculations.

ALERT!

The tax-free withdrawal status for these accounts is currently set to expire on December 31, 2010. If you hold money in a Coverdell account, you should monitor congressional action in this regard. If your child will be attending college after 2010, you may want to consider other vehicles.

Advantages of a Coverdell account

- Earnings are federal income tax free if used for qualified education expenses.
- A wide range of investment choices is allowed.
- Private elementary and secondary school expenses qualify for tax-free withdrawals.

Disadvantages of a Coverdell account

- Asset is assessable for financial aid.
- A 10-percent penalty is levied on earnings if not used for qualified expenses.
- Funds must be distributed within thirty days of the designated beneficiary reaching age thirty.

- Withdrawals made after December 31, 2010, will be taxable unless Congress acts to extend provisions.
- Income limits apply to families earning more than $190,000 or single tax filers earning more than $95,000.

Report Card for Coverdell Account

Financial Aid: A-

Treated as an asset of the account owner for EFC and, therefore, usually assessed at the parents' 5.6 percent rate.

Taxes: A

Earnings are federal income tax free at least until December 31, 2010.

Control: A-

There is a wide range of investment choices, but contributions are limited to $2,000 per year. If funds are not used for qualified education expenses, a 10-percent penalty is assessed on the interest.

---

6. UTMA/UGMA Accounts

Discussed briefly in chapter 5, accounts created under the Uniform Transfers to Minors Act (UTMA) or Uniform Gifts to Minors Act (UGMA) are held in a child's name with a parent or other adult listed as the custodian. Transfers made into these accounts are considered irrevocable gifts. UTMA and UGMA assets commonly include mutual funds, bonds, savings accounts, CDs, and life insurance.

These accounts are ticking financial-aid time bombs. One way to diffuse them is by selling the investments in the UTMA/UGMA and investing the cash in a student-owned UTMA/UGMA 529 plan. However, before doing so you should weigh the tax cost against the potential savings through financial aid.

These accounts should be one of the last options you consider. They should really only be opened by families with extremely high EFCs who won't qualify for need-based financial aid and who want to make unique investments or more actively manage the account. Others should consider a 529 savings plan, which will provide much greater tax benefits.

Advantages of a UTMA/UGMA plan

- Interest, dividends, and capital gains up to $1,800 are taxed at the child's rate; any additional earnings are taxed at the parents' highest rate.
- There are no contribution limits, but gift taxes may apply.
- There are no restrictions on income levels.
- Contributions can be invested how the custodian chooses.

Disadvantages of a UTMA/UGMA plan

- Assets are assessable for EFC calculations at the student's rate.
- Funds transfer automatically to student at age eighteen or twenty-one, depending on state.
- The plan is subject to kiddie tax if an account generates more than $1,800 in income (see chapter 7).

Report Card for a UTMA/UGMA Plan

Financial Aid: F

Assets and income are assessed at the student's rate in EFC calculations.

Taxes: C+

Income is taxed at the student's rate if less than $1,800; any additional income is taxed at the parents' highest rate.

Control: B-

Money can be invested in all common vehicles, and there are no income or contribution limits. When the student reaches eighteen or twenty-one (depending on the state), the custodian loses control.

7. Work-Related Retirement Plans

For older parents, using funds from a work-related retirement plan—whether an employer-sponsored 401(k) or a self-employed Keogh account—has a couple of advantages. First, these plans aren't assessed in the EFC calculations, and, second, money can be withdrawn penalty free at age 59.5. If you were forty when your child was born, your retirement account will probably become available some time in your student's sophomore year.

Advantages of work-related retirement plans

- A wide variety of plans is available, including 401(k)s, 403(b)s, SIMPLE IRAs, SEP IRAs, Solo 401(k)s, Keoghs, and more.
- Asset is non-assessable for financial aid.
- Contributions are tax deductible.
- Earnings are tax deferred.
- Contributions have no income limit.
- Match may be provided by your employer.
- Withdrawals after age 59.5 are penalty free.
- Loans may be taken on certain accounts before age 59.5.
- Money not used for college can remain for retirement.

Disadvantages of work-related retirement plans

- Contribution limitations vary by plan.
- Investment options may be limited.
- Distributions are fully taxable and count as income for financial aid purposes

8. Taxable Investment Accounts

While parents may take some comfort in being able to tell their children, "You own a college savings account," there is absolutely nothing wrong with a standard brokerage or investment account earmarked for college. For families with an extremely high EFC who don't expect to receive need-based financial aid, it makes sense to save in both an investment account and a 529 plan.

If reducing your taxes is a primary goal, there are many other tax-efficient investments from which you can choose,

Report Card for Work Related Retirement Plans

Financial Aid: A

Assets are not assessed for financial aid, but distributions are assessed as income in subsequent years. If used after you have filled out your last financial aid form—January 1 of the student's junior year—there is no impact on financial aid.

Taxes: A

Contributions are tax deductible and growth is tax deferred.

Control: B/A

There are no income limits on these accounts. However, if you are an employee with a 401(k) or 403(b), your investment options may be limited. Business owners with SEP or SIMPLE IRAs usually have a wide variety of investment options.

including index funds, stocks, exchange traded funds, and municipal bonds.

Advantages of taxable investment accounts

- Parents have complete control over assets.
- Contributions can be made regardless of income levels.
- Contributions can be invested however owner chooses.
- Investments may be gifted.
- Money can be easily moved to a non-assessable account before college.

Disadvantages of taxable investment accounts

- Asset is assessable for financial aid.
- Account is fully taxable to owner.

Report Card for Taxable Investment Accounts

Financial Aid: B

Both the value of the investment and the earnings it generates will be assessed in determining your EFC. I give these accounts a B instead of a lower grade because their flexibility allows you to move funds to a non-assessable asset before college.

Taxes: C

Income generated by these accounts is fully taxable. Here, too, their flexibility is a virtue. You can gift appreciated assets to students and let them liquidate investments in their low tax bracket during college years. You can also keep your tax burden low by choosing tax-efficient investments. Moreover, if you hold the investment for longer than one year, you can take advantage of favorable long-term capital gains rates.

Control: A

Because these investments are free of restrictions, you have maximum control. You can invest whatever you have any way you want to. You can liquidate your holdings at any time or gift them to anyone you want.

9. Cash Value Life Insurance

For families that need insurance coverage, have a healthy cash flow, and are seeking an additional tax-efficient vehicle because they are in a high tax bracket, a universal life policy is another option. Unlike term life insurance, these policies have an investment component, so that part of the premium pays for the life insurance while the remainder, or cash value, is invested and grows tax deferred.

Owners of these policies can borrow against the cash value of their investment for college expenses, and although interest may be charged on this loan, withdrawals are not taxable. In addition, the policy is a non-assessable asset for the purpose of financial aid. I should add here that in order for cash value life insurance to work as a college funding vehicle, the policy owner must contribute a significant amount beyond the cost of the insurance portion of the premium. If, for instance, the cost of the insurance is $90 per month and you are paying $100 per month, the amount you save and have available, in other words the cash value, will not go very far in paying for college. (Chapter 11 discusses the role of universal life insurance in a comprehensive financial plan.)

Advantages of cash value life insurance

- Asset is non-assessable for financial aid.
- Growth can be tax deferred and withdrawals tax free through loans.
- Owner has life insurance coverage.
- Contributions can be made regardless of income level.
- Many policies accept large contributions.

Disadvantages of cash value life insurance

- Policy must be maintained properly; over- or under-funding can cause problems.
- Cash-flow commitment to cover insurance costs may be high.
- Policy loans may charge interest.
- Investment options are limited.

Report Card for Cash Value Life Insurance

Financial Aid: A

Cash value life insurance is a non-assessable asset.

Taxes: A

The investment portion grows tax deferred and funds are not taxed when accessed through a loan.

Control: C

When maintained properly, a cash value life insurance policy provides a flexible source of funds for college. However, many of these policies have limited investment options and long waiting periods before investments can be accessed.

---

10. Series EE Bonds

Issued by the federal government, Series EE bonds come in values ranging from $50 to $10,000. Offering low interest levels, this is primarily an investment for the ultraconservative in regard to risk.

They are also assessable assets for calculating your EFC. Unfortunately, many students own EE bonds, and these dramatically increase their EFC. Though there are parents who feel these bonds don't need to be reported because they are kept in a shoebox in the closet, I need to remind them that lying on financial aid forms can subject you to fines.

Earnings on these bonds when used for college are tax free if they fulfill the following conditions:

- The bonds were issued after December 31,1989.
- The bonds were purchased by an individual who was twenty-four years or older.
- The bonds must be used by the taxpayer, or his/her spouse or dependent.
- Single tax filers begin a phaseout of the tax-free status at $61,200 modified adjusted gross income and joint tax filers at $91,850.

More information about savings bonds, including a calculator to determine what your bonds are worth, is available online (www.savingsbonds.com).

Advantages of EE bonds

- Distributions are tax free, subject to restrictions, when used for college expenses.
- Funds can be transferred to a 529 plan without tax consequences.
- Investment risk is low.

Disadvantages of EE bonds

- Distributions can be taxable.

- Asset is assessable for financial aid and may be considered a student's asset if purchased with his or her social security number.
- Investment upside potential is limited.

Report Card for Series EE Bonds

Financial Aid: C

These bonds are assessed at owner's rates, 5.6 percent for parents and at least 20 percent for students.

Taxes: B

Although EE bonds can be used for college tax free, this is only true if all the restrictions listed above are met.

Control: B-

In order to redeem EE bonds, you must be the owner, co-owner, or entitled individual, and the bond must be twelve months old. Although most financial institutions will redeem your bonds for you, you may have to send the bonds to a Federal Reserve Bank for redemption. This can create delays, and more legwork may be required.

In Conclusion

Having presented ten potential investment options, each with its own unique blend of benefits and drawbacks, here is the advice I give my clients. First and foremost, if you have a retirement plan at work that offers a matching contribution, save into the retirement plan at least up to the match. Where else will you get an instant 100 percent return on your investment? Second, if you meet the income limitations, save into a Roth IRA. These vehicles are financial-aid friendly, tax efficient, offer a full range of investment options, and, best of all, can be used for your retirement if not needed for college.

If you have managed all this and still have money to invest, then you should consider a 529 savings plan and/or a regular investment account. I often recommend that my clients contribute to both. In this way you get the tax benefits of the 529 savings plan and the greater selection and liquidity of a conventional account.

Savings provides you with options and flexibility. You are always better off with savings than without. Moreover, you need to save in the right places. You want investment vehicles that can be used to meet college expenses without destroying your chances of receiving financial aid. Finally, you need to position your savings so that whatever is left can be used for your retirement.

ALERT!

As discussed throughout this book, private colleges write their own rules and may ask for disclosure on non-assessable assets. This is rare, and it is rarer still that these accounts are used in their calculations to reduce a financial aid award. Still, it can happen.

10

The Best College at the Right Price

Though it may sound flippant, choosing a college is in many respects like buying a car. Both the name on your student's college sweatshirt and the car you drive say a little something about you. Both cost a lot of money. In shopping for either, some people seek out deals, while others happily pay the sticker price. There are also plenty of people who buy more than they can afford. A lot of families commit to years of high college payments that are well beyond their means even though there are less expensive options available. Does a $50,000 Mercedes provide better transportation than a $20,000 Toyota? It depends on what you mean by better.

Do more expensive and prestigious schools provide a better education and thus a better return on investment for the money?

The answer is not at all clear. If you compare the taste of the cafeteria food and quality of the athletic facilities at a $45,000 private college and at your $10,000 local public college, chances are good that the private college will score higher, just as the interior of a luxury car is more attractive than an economy car.

However, if the question is, "Which school will make my child more successful?" then the answer is less clear. There are plenty of successful, wealthy people in this country who didn't attend Ivy League colleges. In recent years, a large number of articles have questioned whether the high cost of a prestigious college is a good investment. There is certainly no consensus on the answer. I have asked many professionals involved in making hiring decisions about this issue. Here are two points of view that offer somewhat different perspectives.

Steve Kimball, recruiting manager of the hi-tech firm EMC, responded to my question this way.

> Large companies do a lot of recruiting from well-known schools, so try to keep that in mind while making your college selection. Name recognition does count, and it is a factor. However, the best students that I have hired have one common characteristic. They honestly know what they want to do and why they want to do it. The students that just spent $150,000 on their

education and have no clue what they want to do for work stand out like a sore thumb.

Stephen Billhardt, principal of the Patrick S. Cunniff School, looks at the issue differently. This is his response.

> As the cost of private education continues to soar, I would give the advice not to spend one's educational dollars at a private institution, but rather to save those funds for pursuit of a master's degree program at received at a name-brand institution. (Of course, if your funds are extensive, it can't hurt to have a name brand at both the undergraduate and graduate levels.) State universities actually offer broader programs and courses of study than smaller institutions and actually allow students to explore more career choices. Only parents and students, however, can make these decisions. My point, though, is that as an employer, the name of an undergraduate college or university means less and less to me and the overall resume packet is what gets candidates into my office for an interview.

Yet another point of view is offered by the online job site CollegeGrad.com (www.CollegeGrad.com), which reports that the number-one factor in getting a job is the student's major. The second is how a student interviews, and the third is experience. Grade-point average, school attended, and what he or she wears to the interview all score lower.

So, even if there is no definitive answer to the question of how valuable a prestigious school is in terms of employment, one point does stand out. Employers are looking for students who are excited about pursuing a given field. Therefore, those high school students who engage in some sort of career planning and at least understand their interests will be in a better position to choose colleges that support their goals.

Most college counselors agree that students excel when they are in an environment that fits them, regardless of prestige. The challenge is to find the school where your student will apply himself, or where she will get involved on campus.

Tim Lee, president of the Independent Educational Consultants Association and director of Advocates for Human Potential, draws a more detailed picture of this challenge.

> Finding the right college can be a rewarding process, but for some families the experience is challenging, overwhelming, and at times frustrating. With more than three thousand colleges and universities across the country, students today find that there are many options to fit their needs. Many colleges may be well known if not household names. However, students probably will never have heard of a majority of the colleges in existence. Each and every college has something valuable to offer to the

right student. The college that is best for you is the one that meets your needs. You will be happier in a college that fits, and you will also have a much better chance of getting in.

Too often the best college is defined as the most prestigious. But the best match for you is the college that offers a level of academic challenge in line with your ability and preparation, provides an instructional style that matches the way you learn best, offers a major or program of study in line with your interests and needs, provides an environment and sense of community that gives you a sense of belonging, and appreciates you for what you do well.

Charlotte Klaar, founder and director of College Consulting Services, notes that some students need time off before taking the next step and offers some helpful advice.

It is not a disgrace to consider a gap year program or a year of post-graduate study. Nor is it an issue to let your child understand that technical school is still post-secondary learning. All these options should be available to students so that they prepare for their future properly. College is much too expensive a venture to not put in the right kind of preparation or to force on a student whose talents lie in other directions.

This is an important reminder that there are more options for success than graduating from high school and going off to the most expensive college that your student can get into and you can afford. To reiterate, along with a thorough college search, I strongly encourage families do some career planning with their student, evaluating their interests, strengths, and weaknesses.

In addition, don't forget that there are probably many colleges that would be a good fit for your student. Knowing that you have options should take some of the pressure off both parents and students. When families get out from under the extreme pressure of a college search, they make better decisions. In contrast, when families feel they have to choose between one or two high-priced colleges, they are likely to make sacrifices that could be avoided.

Adding Up the Numbers

Before you decide on a college, you need to compare how purchasing four years of a more expensive college will affect your financial picture, and what, if anything, would be lost by choosing a less expensive option. If you've done the work outlined in the previous chapters, you now know what the bottom line will be at each college you are considering. You are no longer looking at the sticker price, but what your actual out-of-pocket commitment will be. There may not be any one obvious right answer, but as the CFO of your family, you can weigh the options and make an informed buying decision.

Now you need to carry your analysis one step further—the step implicit in the title of this book. You need to look at where the actual cash you use to pay for college will come from, and what spending this amount means for your retirement. Not including help from grandparents, you have seven sources to pay tuition bills: financial aid, student's savings, parents' savings, student's income, parents' income, student's borrowing, and parents' borrowing.

By utilizing the strategies previously mentioned to obtain as much financial aid as possible, you have chipped away at the total cost of college. Unfortunately, after that, you have only the remaining six resources. There are no more freebies.

I suggest you create a page or spreadsheet, as illustrated in table 9, for each college. If you fill in the numbers and the total at the bottom is less than the total at the top, then (1) you haven't finished the job, (2) the amount of borrowing required is beyond your comfort level, or (3) the expenses are truly out of your reach.

Paying from Savings

After financial aid, a family will then have to rely on its own resources, and since most students have very little set aside for college, these savings come for the most part out of parents' pockets.

This is where you need to weigh the amount you allocate to college against the amount you save for retirement. Following is a

Table 9

Paying for College

Cost of Attendance: $ _____ per year

Year in College	First	Second	Third	Fourth
Financial Aid				
Student's Savings				
Parents' Savings				
Student's Income				
Parents' Income				
Student's Borrowing				
Parents' Borrowing				
Total Funds Available				

scenario that takes this conflict out of the realm of the abstract. I take a hypothetical family, the Nicolsons, make some assumptions, and then project the impact on their retirement savings of paying for an expensive private college versus their in-state public college. No doubt the assumptions I make in this scenario will differ from your circumstances—I have simplified the picture to make it easier to follow—but you can use this method to estimate the impact of a similar scenario on your financial picture.

Mr. and Mrs. Nicolson are both fifty years old and hope to retire at sixty-five. They each earn $40,000 year, and they are able to save 10 percent of their annual income in their investment portfolio. Their portfolio—consisting of funds from an inheritance as well as their continued savings—is now worth $260,000. Feeling blessed by their recent windfall, they feel privileged to have the ability to pay all of their daughter's college expenses and, therefore, do not apply for any financial aid.

Here are more details of the Nicolsons' situation. Keep in mind that while the Nicolsons' numbers and circumstances are simpler than most real families, the point is to see the impact of different college expenses.

- The Nicolsons hope to have $64,000 a year in income after they retire (80 percent of their current income).

- They assume their salaries will increase about 3 percent annually until they retire.

- They expect an 8-percent return on their investments before retirement.

- Planning to invest more conservatively after retirement, they then expect a 6-percent return on their savings.

- Inflation averages 3 percent during their lifetime.

- They receive no financial aid for college.

- They will receive Social Security benefits in retirement.

- Being debt averse, the Nicolsons insist that all college payments be made from their savings, and to simplify matters they decide to pay all four years of college up front.

When getting ready to make their decision, the Nicolsons need to do some math and project how long their money will last after retirement if they pay for the $45,000-a-year private college (see table 10) or the $15,000-a-year public (see table 11).

Table 10

Paying Private-College Tuition

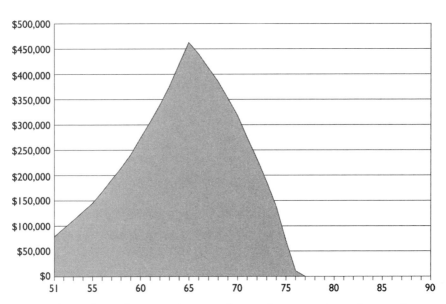

Much to their dismay, the Nicolsons discover that if everything works out as planned, they will completely run out of money at age seventy-six, after having paid $180,000 up front for their daughter's college education (according to Bankrate.com's retirement calculator). Of course, they don't know how long they will live or what their health will be like in their declining years, but this is certainly not a scenario they would choose.

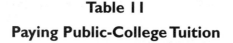

Table 11
Paying Public-College Tuition

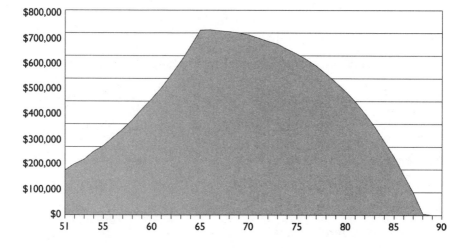

In this scenario, paying $60,000 up front for college, the Nicolsons' money lasts until they are eighty-eight years old.

In comparing these two scenarios I am not suggesting that families should hoard their money, or that they should always look for the least expensive college they can find. What I want to show, however, is how $120,000 difference in out-of-pocket expenses can dramatically affect the financial future of parents. In this case, the difference would allow the Nicolsons to live twelve additional years in retirement without going broke. Hence, your college commitments could be the difference between a comfortable retirement and a difficult financial struggle.

Paying from Income and/or by Borrowing

After figuring in financial aid and the depletion of their savings, many families find that they have to make up the difference by squeezing money out of their current income and/or by borrowing. I treat these together because they represent an ongoing source of cash you don't already have in hand.

By subtracting your monthly expenses from your monthly income, you can see at a glance how much of your earnings you can earmark for college. It also shows how much you would need to borrow to make up the difference and how much your monthly payments would run on the loan.

Table 12 illustrates the monthly payment required to repay loans of different amounts using standard loan amortization over ten years at two different interest rates. Of course, the rates currently available to you may be higher or lower. You should ask your loan officer for an amortization table and be sure you understand all the conditions of any loan you take.

Seeing the actual monthly payments is a great help in evaluating how much of a loan you and your student want to take on. When thinking about how you will pay for college, it can be deceptively easy to simply say, "Oh, we will just borrow to make up the difference," or, "Our savings will cover that amount." It's a completely different story when you see how the actual numbers play out, either in terms of your loan payments or your retirement options.

With this information in hand, I hope you will go back over the strategies presented throughout this book to see if you can wring

Table 12
Monthly Loan Payments

Estimated student loan payments at 6.8 percent (standard Stafford loan rate) with a ten-year term	Estimated parent loan payments at 8.5 percent (standard PLUS loan rate) with a ten-tear term
$10,000 = $115/month	$10,000 = $124/month
$20,000 = $230/month	$20,000 = $248/month
$40,000 = $460/month	$40,000 = $496/month
$60,000 = $690/month	$60,000 = $744/month
$80,000 = $921/month	$80,000 = $992/month
$100,000 = $1,151/month	$100,000 = $1,250/month

out further savings and/or a little more financial aid for what will be one of the major expenses of your life. I also suggest that you take the time to look more closely at your current finances to see if you can save more than you do today. If you can increase the amount and put your savings on a regular schedule, you will have more options down the road. Finally, evaluate your student's college choice in conjunction with your retirement plan. Weigh the pros and cons of each school and try to best determine where your student will thrive and succeed. Carefully consider, as a CFO would, the investment required by you for each college choice, because this decision will likely impact your retirement.

11

Comprehensive Planning

I frequently conduct workshops and seminars where I ask parents how they are going to pay for college. The five most common answers run something like this.

"We plan on getting scholarships."

"I guess we are going to have to borrow."

"Financial aid hopefully."

"Probably out of pocket."

And my favorite, "That is why I am here."

Whether your student gets a free ride, a little financial aid, a lot of financial aid, help from grandparents, or expects to pay

100 percent of the total cost of college, a comprehensive plan will help. Developing a plan and sticking to it makes you efficient and focused.

This is exactly what a good CFO does when presented with the finances of a company or a household. There aren't any magic formulas that will send your child to school for free, but committing to this process will give you an overview of what to expect and more control over your household finances.

The vast majority of American families—whether they get financial aid or not—find themselves faced with bills for many thousands of dollars during their children's college years. Having a real financial plan in hand will help you do the following.

- Know how much discretionary cash flow you can allocate to college payments
- Develop efficient exit strategies out of your investments
- Find the best ways to borrow
- Create efficient systems for managing your investments
- Understand how assuming various college costs will affect your own financial goals, especially your retirement

In this chapter I will explore and explain the larger financial context around college planning. A comprehensive family financial plan usually addresses six areas: cash flow, investments, retirement, college, insurance, and taxes. While most of this book focuses on the techniques and tools of college planning, the following pages look at how these other areas influence your decisions about college and how the impact of paying for college may affect them. The purpose is come up with the best way to handle your finances before, through, and after the college years.

Cash Flow

Almost every financial decision you make is directly linked to your family's income. If you are like most people, you have a pretty clear idea of what comes into your household on an annual basis. Very few families, though, ever analyze their expenses. Perhaps they are afraid to. Nevertheless, only when you know what is left over at the end of every month can you begin to control your cash flow and use it efficiently. If you don't look carefully at how you spend money and have never developed a conscious plan for investing your excess dollars, those dollars have an uncanny tendency to disappear.

Whether they are making $30,000 or $300,000, people tend to spend what they earn. Part of my job as a financial planner is to analyze a family's cash flow. When I finish the paperwork, I often find that people should have money left over at the end of each month, and I point this out to them. Usually their response is either to laugh or to look very disturbed. They see from my calculations that they have discretionary income, but they have no idea where the money is going or has gone.

That's when I introduce them to one of the most powerful financial planning tools available, a form of disciplined savings usually referred to as "paying yourself first." It's the simplest of concepts and strategies. All it requires is for you to consistently set aside a specific amount of money every month, yet it's the surest formula for financial success over time. Moreover, it doesn't require a great deal of discipline or self-restraint. All you need to do is set up an automatic transfer of a portion of your paycheck to an account earmarked for the goal you choose.

While most people start by believing they don't have enough money to begin a savings program, it's amazing how easily families adjust. Then, just a couple of years later, they look at their investment statement and see that they have achieved savings they had previously thought impossible. I've seen it again and again.

Table 13 is a simple income and expense worksheet you can use to determine your own discretionary income. You can use this as a model or create your own if your situation requires extra lines or different categories.

Table 13

Income and Expense Worksheet

Income	
First Income Source	$
Second Income Source	$
Other Income	$
Total Monthly Income	$
Expenses	
Monthly Savings	$
Federal Taxes	$
State Taxes	$

Property Taxes	$
Mortgage/Rent Payment	$
Home/Rent Insurance Payment	$
Utilities	$
Telephone	$
Home Improvements	$
Auto Payments	$
Auto Insurance Payments	$
Auto Maintenance	$
Life Insurance Premiums	$
Disability Insurance Premiums	$
Health Insurance Premiums	$
Education Costs	$
Medical Costs	$
Loan/Debt Payments	$
Gifts to Charities	$
Travel	$
Food/Groceries	$
Clothing	$
Personal Care (Hair Care/Dry Cleaning)	$
Cable TV	$
Entertainment and Recreation	$
Other	$
Other	$
Other	$
Total Monthly Expenses	$
Total Discretionary Cash Flow	$
(Total monthly income minus total monthly expenses)	$

Fill in your worksheet as accurately as you can, looking back at your checkbook or credit card statements to make sure that the numbers you are using truly reflect what you are spending and what you are earning. Once you have accounted for as many items as you can, subtract your total monthly expenses from your monthly income. The balance is your discretionary cash flow. Now you need to capture those dollars and apply them to the goal of your choosing, whether it be a college payment plan or a Roth IRA. Taking that first step is hard, and it does require some degree of discipline to save a consistent amount each and every month until it becomes automatic. If you run into snags, go back to your income and expense worksheet to see what has changed.

Investment Planning

Think of your investment portfolio as your own personal business. You put money into it on a regular basis with the ultimate goal of being able to live off of the income it generates in the future. Business owners put a lot of energy into managing their businesses because they know their livelihoods depend on their efforts, and they know they can't take extended vacations from this responsibility. When it comes to managing your portfolio, however, it's easy to get distracted. You have a day job. Your family needs your attention. Your home needs a new roof.

Nevertheless, the success or failure of your investments could have a huge impact—maybe even more than the amount of financial aid you receive—on how well you can handle the expenses of sending your children to college. A vast amount is written about how to choose and manage your investments, and I recommend that everyone educate themselves on the subject, whether they have a small or a large amount to invest, and whether they intend to work with a professional or handle it themselves. While the subject is too large to even begin to explore here, there are four areas that I think need to be mentioned. Improving your performance in even one of these areas can have a dramatic positive impact on your retirement plan.

Asset Allocation

The key to successful investing, like many other endeavors, is to have a goal and a plan. The biggest investment mistakes are made when people let emotions dictate their decisions and deviate from their original game plan.

Every investment prospectus contains a disclaimer that says, "Past performance is no guarantee of future results." In other words, things don't always work out as you expect. That's why the first word in investing is usually "diversification." Because markets are unpredictable, it's important to have a combination of investments that might include mutual funds, exchange traded funds (commonly referred to as ETFs), individual stocks, bonds, and real estate.

Two famous investment studies analyzed the performance of large pension plans over different decades. In both studies they concluded that the primary factor in determining a plan's performance was attributable to its asset allocation policy—for instance, the relative percent of stocks and bonds it held—rather than the particular stocks and bonds contained in the portfolio.

The key information in this for you as an individual investor is that coming up with a sound asset allocation plan coupled with a disciplined investment program gives you the best chance for success over time. For example, the years 2000 and 2001 were tough for a lot of investors, especially those who held a large portion of their portfolio in large capitalization growth stocks and technology stocks. However, according to American Century Investment's "Periodic Table of Style Rotation," those investors holding small capitalization value stocks and real estate stocks were up by double digits both years instead of being down by double digits. Investors in these asset classes didn't have to choose one fund over another, or time their buys and sells to make money in those tough markets; simply holding a broad array of assets, or having exposure to a range of asset classes, led to healthier portfolios.

The range of asset classes includes but is not limited to:

- Cash
- Large-capitalization (large-cap) domestic growth stocks
- Large-capitalization (large-cap) domestic value stocks
- Middle-capitalization (mid-cap) domestic growth stocks
- Middle-capitalization (mid-cap) domestic value stocks
- Small-capitalization (small-cap) domestic growth stocks
- Small-capitalization (small-cap) domestic value stocks
- International large-cap growth stocks
- International large-cap value stocks

- International small- and mid-cap growth stocks
- International small- and mid-cap value stocks
- Real estate stocks
- Precious metals
- Commodities
- Government bonds
- Corporate bonds
- High-yield bonds
- International bonds

It's important to understand two terms that have special meaning when used in relation to stock investments: "growth" and "value." Growth investors believe in buying stocks with above-average earnings no matter what the price. Value investors look exclusively for bargains stocks that are trading at less than their usual valuation. An analogy to real estate investing may further clarify the difference. Growth investors can be compared to real estate investors who flip properties. They look for real estate in high growth areas and ride the momentum of the marketplace to sell for a profit. In contrast, value real estate investors purchase properties in a slow or declining market where properties are undervalued. It may take some time for a particular market to recover, but when it does, the value investor reaps the benefits.

Which strategy is better? That is highly debatable. What we do know is that each style tends to be successful at different times. For example, growth investing was the best approach in the late 1990s, while value investing has been more successful through the early 2000s. Most financial advisors recommend developing a portfolio with a combination of both growth and value to create greater diversity and reduce risk.

While most people assume that investing means buying stocks, the truth is that the bond market is vastly larger than the stock market. Moreover, there are numerous types of bonds available. Getting acquainted with these options will help you diversify your portfolio. For those who are completely new to the concept, it is important to know that when you buy a bond you are lending money to the institution that issued it, which may be a company, the federal government, or some local or state agency. The borrower promises to return your money on a specific date; until that time, it pays you a stated rate of interest. Bonds vary in the rate of interest they pay as well as the financial stability of the issuer.

Federal bonds are IOUs issued with "the full faith and backing" of the U.S. government, and even here there are a variety of choices, including Treasury Bonds, Treasury Inflation Protected Securities (TIPS), and Government National Mortgage Association (Ginnie Mae) bonds, among others. Local governments also issue bonds, often referred to as municipal bonds, which are attractive to those in higher income tax brackets because they generate tax-exempt interest. Corporate bonds are issued by public and private businesses. These carry a higher risk of default, but they may also pay a higher interest rate. High-yield bonds are corporate bonds that carry the highest interest rates on the market, but because the businesses that issue them are considered unstable, they come with greater risk. Finally, there are International Bonds issued by foreign governments and/or foreign corporations.

When creating a portfolio, the first task is to decide what percentage of your money you want to allocate to each asset class. How much you place in these categories will depend on your age, the number of years to your retirement, your tax bracket, and your risk tolerance. After you determine the percentages, you can then decide on specific investments in each category. For most individuals, it won't make sense to hold all eighteen asset classes listed above. Conventional wisdom suggests combining some of these categories, placing all bonds in one category and all U.S. stocks in another, to create four asset classes. This will simplify the process and help you get started in developing a portfolio. As your portfolio grows, you can always increase the complexity by adding categories.

Here is a very simplified approach to creating a portfolio—following a model developed by MFS Investment Management—that utilizes four different approaches and four asset classes.

1. **Conservative Portfolio:** 50 percent bonds, 35 percent U.S. stocks, 10 percent cash, 5 percent international stocks

2. **Moderate Portfolio:** 50 percent U.S. stocks, 35 percent bonds, 10 percent international stocks, 5 percent cash

3. **Growth Portfolio:** 60 percent U.S. stocks, 20 percent bonds, 20 percent International stocks

4. **Aggressive Growth Portfolio:** 80 percent U.S. stocks, 20 percent international stocks

Within the preceding models, MFS typically holds eight to ten mutual funds, which can be mirrored by individual investors.

For example, a conservative portfolio might hold three different bond funds to satisfy the 50 percent requirement, three different U.S. stock funds to make up the 35 percent requirement, one cash fund, and one international stock fund.

A basic asset allocation calculator is available online for free at the CCH website (www.finance.cch.com) along with a number of useful financial calculators. Calculators such as the one offered by CCH suggest an asset allocation formula based on the variables you enter.

Asset allocations usually appear in a pie chart like the one below.

Table 14

Sample Asset Allocation Pie Chart

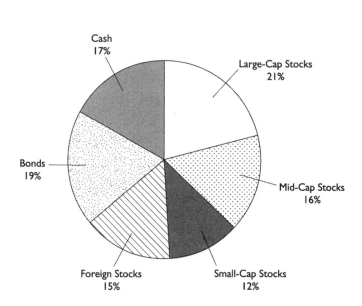

Some online asset allocation programs (typically found through subscription services) allow you to compare your current portfolio and the recommended portfolio on the basis of risk and expected return. These comparisons produce three possible results.

1. The recommended portfolio has a lower risk value and a lower return value than your current portfolio. Why would you want a lower projected return? Well, no one wants that, but depending on what your risk tolerance, the software may determine that your asset allocation puts you at greater risk than you realize. This is important information because, being risk adverse, if your portfolio is exposed to extreme fluctuations, you are likely to make emotional, and therefore usually poor, investment decisions.

2. The recommended portfolio has a higher risk value and a higher return value than your current portfolio. Why would someone want to take on more risk? Well, if you are forty years old and expect to retire in twenty-five years, and all your money is in cash or bonds, you certainly have room to be more aggressive as well as the ability to ride out any temporary setbacks. If your portfolio is too conservative in relation to your personality, situation, and goals, this is the advice an asset allocation program would give you.

3. The recommended portfolio has a lower risk value and a higher return value than your current portfolio. While you would hate to be told that your portfolio has been underperforming,

it's great to know going forward that you can do better. In fact, this situation is more common than you might think. A lot of people have inefficient portfolios that produce poor returns for the amount of risk they are taking.

Here's an example of how a better asset allocation can make a huge difference in just a few years.

From January 1, 2000, to December 31, 2004, Kelly Kannapiran kept her IRA savings in a portfolio of three mutual funds, two large-cap mutual funds and one "balanced" mutual fund that invests in both stocks and bonds. The results described below represent actual results for the specific years for the funds in her portfolio. While the stock market gives varying returns during different years and cycles, a good asset allocation strategy should produce better returns over the long run.

Looking at Kelly's portfolio I noticed she had a one-year return of 4.71 percent and a reasonable three-year average annual return of 10.96 percent. However, due to the bear market of the early 2000s, her five-year average annual return was a negative 2.68 percent. Wanting a portfolio that could better weather a bear market, Kelly asked for some recommendations. I entered the kind of personal factors discussed above into the program and came up with a much more diversified portfolio. Here were her new recommended allocations:

- 10 percent short-term bond funds
- 17 percent long- and intermediate-term bonds
- 6 percent high-yield bond funds
- 32 percent large-cap stock funds

- 7.5 percent mid-cap stock funds
- 7.5 percent small-cap stock funds
- 13 percent international stock funds
- 7 percent real estate funds

Though applying hindsight feels unfair, I have done so to illustrate the difference a healthy asset allocation would have made for Kelly. Had she invested in index funds in the percentages recommended for each asset class, her returns during the same five years would have looked a lot better. With her new portfolio she would have earned 8.81 percent on a one-year time frame and would have had a three-year annual average return of 13.75 percent. In addition, her five-year return, although not earthshaking, would still have been a positive 5.11 percent per year.

Comparing the two portfolios, you can see that if Kelly Kannapiran started with $80,000, five years later the value would have shrunk to $69,839 with her original portfolio. In contrast, her recommended portfolio in that same five-year period would have been worth $102,638. The difference, commonly referred to as the opportunity cost, is $32,799.

Term to know ▶	*Opportunity Cost*

> The opportunity cost is the lost potential gain when choosing one alternative over another, or, more narrowly, what you lose when you make a less than optimal choice.

Over a span of five years, the difference between an inefficient portfolio and a well-designed portfolio could easily be equivalent to a full year's tuition, even if you begin with a modest amount. And while Kelly Kannapiran may be only a name in a book to you, if you have a child who is a senior in high school today, it will be that same five-year time frame before he or she graduates from college. How will you handle your investments in that time? What will your opportunity costs be?

It should be emphasized in this example that Kelly's recommended portfolio not only achieved greater returns over one, three, and five years, but it also did so with less risk.

Overlapping Investments

One final observation about Kelly's portfolio is that she made the mistake of choosing overlapping investments. In other words, though she owned several mutual funds, these funds contained many of the same stocks. Thus, she had the illusion rather than the reality of diversifying her investments.

In fact, hers is a common mistake. Many investors fail to realize that their mutual funds hold overlapping investments, or that their choice of stocks will thrive or fall together under certain market conditions. If you hold five different mutual funds, but they all invest in the same or similar stocks, you are not reducing your overall risk. In addition, when choosing mutual funds, you need to look below the surface. Sometimes a fund's name doesn't accurately reflect the makeup of its portfolio. Bottom line: seek investments in different kinds of stocks and different asset classes.

Poor Investment Vehicles

Good asset allocation and good diversification doesn't always equate to quality investments. You can have the right kind of fund but not the right stocks or the right funds.

The process of researching and selecting stocks is far beyond the scope of this book. For those who are interested in learning more, I suggest a few books in the resource section at the end of this book. I can also recommend a few free online sources, including Yahoo! Finance (finance.yahoo.com) and Microsoft's MSN Money (moneycentral.msn.com). The MSN Money website has a tool called "StockScouter" that can help you evaluate the quality of your current holdings. I also like Louis Navellier's "Portfoliograder Pro" (found at www.getrichwithgrowth.com), which grades stocks on a scale of A through F.

While these resources can help in the laborious process of researching individual securities, most investors will rely on mutual funds, which are pools of money managed by professionals. Each fund is defined by the kind of assets it holds and the style of investing if follows. Thus, there are large-cap value funds, short-term bond funds, and so forth.

Among the prime benefits of investing through mutual funds are liquidity, diversification, and the active participation of professional managers. Rather than trying to evaluate which stocks you should buy and sell, you have an experienced manager do this for you. In addition, mutual funds are entirely liquid. If you want to sell your shares, you can, and you can have your money in cash within twenty-four hours. Most important, mutual funds instantly provide diversification among numerous stocks and/ or bonds. This diversification not only reduces risk in your portfolio, but also saves on trading costs. Finally, mutual funds are probably the most widely available investment tool in your own retirement plan at work and/or state-sponsored college savings account.

Since there are more than ten thousand mutual funds offered by hundreds of different mutual fund companies, how do you determine which ones to purchase? Once again, this a subject for specialized books, but the Microsoft and Yahoo sites mentioned earlier have mutual fund screeners, which allow you to select specific variables to narrow your search.

Here are some criteria developed from the Yahoo Finance site. You can start with these and fine-tune your list later.

- Choose a specific asset class (U.S. Large Cap Growth or International Bonds, and so forth). This will filter only those funds that meet your asset class need.
- Choose a fund that has a manager with a track record—a tenure of five years or longer.
- Select for a Morningstar rating of four stars or better. Morningstar is the most recognized mutual fund rating organization. It ranks funds within each specific asset class on a scale of one to five stars. Although the science is not perfect, Morningstar's rating will at least narrow your field.
- Select a minimum return rating of "average." This score is computed by Morningstar as well.
- Choose a maximum Morningstar risk rating of "average."

By using these five criteria to narrow your choices, you will have a focused list of funds with experienced management that have performed better than average in terms of risk and return. If your list is still too long, you can apply more criteria, filtering funds by expense ratios, size, and/or recent performance.

Here is an example of how someone might go through the process of improving his portfolio.

Gabe Fisk has a 401(k) with $150,000 currently saved in it. He is fifty years old and has a high tolerance for risk. An asset allocation calculation suggests that he should hold 20 percent of his portfolio in international stocks and 80 percent in domestic stocks. Because he already has money in domestic mutual funds but nothing in international, he consults his benefits guide to determine which mutual funds are available that fulfill his need. Three are listed: Fidelity Overseas, Blackrock International, and Janus Overseas.

Gabe's next step is to go online for more information about each fund. At Yahoo! Finance he sees that Fidelity Overseas has a three-star rating from Morningstar and that its portfolio manager has been in his position for less than two years. The Blackrock International fund has a one-star rating and its portfolio manager has also been in place for less than two years. Finally, he looks at the Janus Overseas fund and sees that it has a five-star rating. In addition, its manager has been at the helm for six and a half years. While knowing that relative standings can change over time, he feels good about choosing the Janus fund.

Gabe's task was relatively simple because his choices were limited. For your IRAs and non-retirement brokerage accounts, instead of three options, you might have thousands. This can be good or bad news depending on whether you like to do research. In either case, the process will be the same—to winnow your choices, selecting promising funds or stocks or bonds, and to maintain an asset allocation that suits your goals and needs. Finally, you need to monitor your selections periodically to make sure that your investment vehicles are continuing to perform well and to rebalance your portfolio if the allocated proportions have changed.

If you feel uncomfortable making these decisions on your own, you can hire a financial planner. You can also invest in one of the asset allocation portfolios offered by the large mutual fund companies. You tell the company how aggressive you want to be, and the company will create and manage a portfolio of eight to ten funds in various asset classes. This is a good option for those who like one-stop shopping and don't want the burden of monitoring their investments.

Poor Investment Behavior

The "Quantitative Analysis of Investor Behavior," an annual research report issued by the research firm DALBAR, Inc., reported that from 1984 to 2003 the average equity investor earned a 2.57 percent annual return while the annual return for the S&P 500 (a commonly used index of large-cap stocks) was 12.2 percent. What could possibly lead so many people to do so badly? In a nutshell, the answer is undisciplined behavior—people chasing hot investments, buying high and selling low. The remedy is simply to choose an asset allocation and stick with it.

After that, your maintenance involves rebalancing your portfolio on either a semi-annual or annual basis. Since some of your investments will grow faster than others, over time they will no longer reflect the asset allocation formula you originally adopted. If and when the markets turn, this imbalance might work against you. By rebalancing periodically, you even out the risk. In addition, since you are selling some assets from those that have grown and buying those that have lagged, you are automatically selling high and buying low.

Let's return to Gabe Fisk for a moment and assume that in the year following his purchase of an international stock fund there was a major run-up in the value of these stocks. Now, instead of representing 20 percent of his portfolio, his international mutual fund accounts for 40 percent. To maintain the proper balance, he sells some of the international stock fund and puts the money into domestic stock funds.

Put this way, it sounds easy. However, most people do the opposite. Having seen international stocks make such gains, they buy these stocks, or, if they have seen gains in an asset, they hold onto it. More often than not, individual investors sell their poor performing assets and buy more of their best performing asset classes. This is why they underperform the market.

The following quote is posted on the website of the U.S. Securities and Exchange Commission (www.sec.gov):

> Stick with your plan: buy low, sell high. Shifting money away from an asset category when it

is doing well in favor of an asset category that is doing poorly may not be easy, but it can be a wise move. By cutting back on the current "winners" and adding more of the current so-called "losers," rebalancing forces you to buy low and sell high.

This point is made somewhat dramatically on the website of the MFS family of mutual funds (www.mfs.com). It describes three different investors who each invested $10,000 on December 31 every year for twenty years from 1986 through 2006 creating a total outlay of $200,000. The money of each was distributed among six asset classes: the Lehman Brothers Aggregate Bond Index; the Morgan Stanley International (MSCI) EAFE (Europe, Australasia, Far East) Index; the Russell 1000 Index; the Russell 1000 Growth index; the Russell 1000 Value Index; and the Russell 2500 Index.

Investor number one chased performance. Each year he invested in the previous year's best performing market segment. Investor number two went for the rebound. Each year she invested in the previous year's worst-performing market segment, hoping for a rebound the next year. Investor number three created a diversified portfolio and rebalanced the assets each year so that they stayed equally distributed among the six asset classes. After twenty years investor one's portfolio was worth $537,207. Investor two had $621,115, and investor three $668,990

The moral of the story is clear: diversify using an appropriate asset allocation formula, select quality investments, and rebalance on a regular basis. A simple systematic plan will not only give you more peace of mind, it will also better help you reach your retirement goals.

Retirement Planning

Close your eyes and picture your youngest child walking across the stage and receiving her diploma. You take some pictures and then you all go out to eat at a local restaurant. Afterward, you drop her off at her apartment and congratulate her one more time. After your goodbyes, you head home. That night you lay your head down on your pillow and take a deep breath. Ah, your last child has made it through college, and you have no more tuition payments. Now what?

Financially speaking, maybe the answer to "now what" is nothing. However, eventually you will have to answer the inevitable question: have I saved enough or am I saving enough to retire and live as I would like to without running out of money in my later years?

This question expresses the underlying concern that informs this book. Because college is such a huge expense that occurs so close to retirement age, it's important that you ask what you want for yourself while you are also trying to figure out how to pay for your children's education. Once you do that, you may be able to come up with a financial game plan that doesn't undermine your best interests.

If you have never tried to calculate what you will need for retirement, I suggest beginning by using an online retirement calculator. I like the easy-to-use calculator provided by Bankrate.com, under their retirement planner tab (found under "calculators" at www. bankrate.com). To come up with a reasonable retirement projection, you will typically need to assemble the following information:

- Amount you have saved and earmarked for retirement
- Amount you are currently saving for retirement
- Amount your employer is giving toward your retirement through matching contributions or profit-sharing
- Amount your company pension will pay
- Amount Social Security will pay
- Monthly income you want in retirement
- Age when you would like to retire
- Assumed growth rates on your assets
- Assumed inflation rate
- Estimate of current and future tax brackets

Arriving at some of these figures may involve assumptions and projections that can seem overwhelming. However, the important thing, to paraphrase Woody Allen, is to show up and do the exercise. Don't be afraid to discover that you are off track. Whatever the results, you can do many things to improve your situation.

Take the example of Erik and Alison Beaurpere, who have just finished paying for their son Matt's final year of college. Both are fifty years old and would like to retire at age sixty-five. Erik, a software engineer, has been saving $4,500 each year into his 401(k), which now has a value of $90,000. Alison, a nurse, has saved $2,000 each year into her 403(b), which is worth $22,000 at present. They both expect to receive Social Security and hope to have a combined income of $75,000 a year after they retire. This amount would represent 75 percent of their current household income. The Beaurpere's assume an average rate of return of 8 percent before retirement and 6 percent after retirement. They also assume that inflation will remain constant at 3 percent.

Not knowing whether their retirement goal is feasible given what they have saved and are saving, they plug their numbers into a retirement calculator and are told that their money is likely to run out by the time they reach eighty-two. The following graph tracks the Beaurperes' savings before retirement and the gradual depletion of those savings after they retire.

Table 15
The Beaurperes' Retirement Outlook

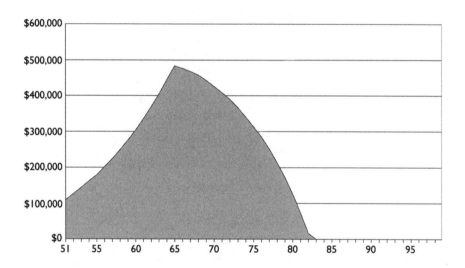

Knowing that Alison's family has a history of longevity, they conclude that they have to make their money last longer. Although Erik cringes at the thought of tightening his belt, they conclude that they have to save more money before retiring. Fortunately they have a way to do so. For the last four years they have been paying $12,000 out of their earnings for Matt's college expenses. They therefore decide to commit this amount to their retirement accounts in addition to what they had already been saving.

Table 16

The Beaurperes' Retirement Outlook With Added Saving

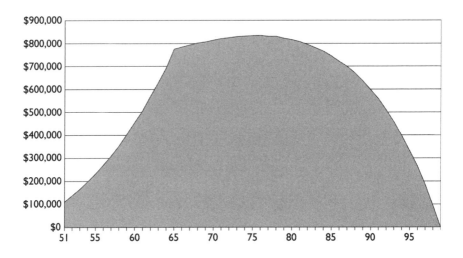

Now the calculator tells them their money will last until they are ninety-nine. The next day they modify their automatic savings plan at work to increase the amount they save out of each paycheck. Now the Beaurperes' sleep better knowing that Matt has graduated, and they will be able to retire in comfort.

Insurance

It's said that people would rather go to the dentist than discuss or buy insurance. Nevertheless, there is no more important time to address this issue than just before your children start college. If you are close to your peak income years, with the expense of college right before you, this is the time to provide a backup. Could you pay for college if you or your spouse died or became disabled? I understand it can be a difficult topic to address, but on the positive side, once you deal with it, you won't have to revisit your decisions for a long time.

In the context of a comprehensive financial plan, two major categories—life insurance and disability insurance—are usually considered key elements. Of the two, life insurance is naturally the most emotionally charged. It involves a choice you make to protect your family in the event of your death. You can compute how much money your family would need if you were gone, but the emotional loss can't be quantified. On one hand, if you don't want to leave anything for your family, that's up to you. On the other hand, if you want to create generational wealth, that's your choice as well. I suggest you and your spouse discuss how you feel about these issues before getting quotes and signing papers.

Life insurance comes in many different forms, each with many variables, but there are four major types of life insurance policies that every consumer should understand.

1. **Term Insurance.** This is the simplest and most common form of life insurance. There is no investment component to this type of coverage. It is, in a way, similar to renting a home instead of buying it. You don't build any equity in this type of policy. When you purchase term insurance you buy coverage for a specific dollar amount and a set length of time and term—say $500,000 for ten years. If you die during that time, your family will receive the specified amount. Otherwise, at the end of the term the policy expires, and you stop paying premiums.

2. **Whole Life Insurance.** Instead of selecting a period of time to be covered, a whole life policy pays a death benefit no matter when you die. The premiums are usually much higher than for a term policy, but unlike term policies, a whole life policy builds equity, commonly referred to as the cash value. Premium payments consist of a baseline insurance cost and an additional amount that is typically invested in bonds and mortgages. The money in the cash account can be used to help pay the premiums in later years, and you can borrow against it, though this borrowing may be subject to fees and interest.

3. **Universal Life Insurance.** Universal life policies are similar to whole life policies but are more flexible because they allow you to change the premium and even the death benefit. You can overfund the cash value account one year and underfund it the next if the cash value is large enough to pay the cost of the insurance. Purchasers of these policies, however, need to be aware of the danger of underfunding. If at any time the cash value of such a policy doesn't cover the insurance costs,

the policy may lapse. When this occurs, the owner may need to apply for a new policy.

4. **Variable Universal Life Insurance.** These policies are similar to universal life in structure but offer the possibility of investing in stock funds, bond funds, and other assets. With these policies you have the ability to grow your cash value faster than whole life and universal life policies. Of course, these same investments can lose money, in which case you may have to increase your premium payments to keep the policy in force.

I generally recommend term life insurance because it's easier to fit in to a tight budget and serves a very specific purpose, such as insuring that your children's college will be paid for if you are not around. It works well as the primary form of coverage for many families. The other three options are usually used for estate planning purposes. They may also be suitable for young families who have time to let the cash value grow, have a good income, and are already funding other tax-favored vehicles.

If you feel that you should have life insurance but haven't acted yet, your first job is to decide how much coverage you want to purchase. The following scenario illustrates the main issues you will want to consider.

Avery and Samantha Banks are both forty-five years old. They have three children, aged ten, twelve, and fourteen. They expect that all their children will attend college. Avery earns $75,000 a year working for a publishing company. Samantha earns $50,000 annually as an architect. They would both like to retire at age sixty-five. They have $65,000 in savings at present. For planning purposes, they assume their savings will grow at an average annual rate of 8 percent, and they assume that inflation will continue at 3 percent. If something were to happen to either of them, they want their life insurance to cover the following expenses.

- Their $300,000 mortgage
- $25,000 in car loans
- $10,000 for funeral expenses
- Their children's college education at $100,000 each
- Enough extra to replace a portion of the deceased's income

Using the insurance calculator found online at Yahoo! Finance, they find that to meet their desires, Avery would need to purchase $1,232,000, and Samantha $901,000. This may be a surprisingly large amount, but keep in mind that replacing lost income is often the variable that creates the largest need. A rule of thumb says that you can safely withdraw 5 percent annually from a lump sum of money to maintain the capital. Therefore, if you want an additional $25,000 in yearly income, you may need an additional lump sum of $500,000 to provide that income (5% X $500,000 = $25,000).

Because their needs are large, I would recommend to the Bankses that they look into the cost of a twenty-year term policy for each. This would take the surviving spouse to retirement age. If the premiums on such policies are too high, they can weigh the option of fifteen-year term policies, which would at least provide coverage until their last child graduates from college. At a bare minimum, they should consider policies with benefits high enough to cover their debts while leaving some excess money that could be used for college expenses. Such a policy wouldn't replace a portion of the diseased spouse's income, but at least it would be a help. The most important point here is that Avery and Samantha need to evaluate their insurance needs now. Because insurance gets more expensive with age, it will never be as affordable as it is today.

In addition to life insurance, most people need to consider disability insurance. After all, your greatest asset may not be your home or your 401(k) but your ability to work and earn a living. If you were unable to bring in a consistent income stream, how would you even begin to make the mortgage payments, save for retirement, or pay for your children's college? And while it's easy to ignore this possibility when you're healthy, the statistics are a bit scary. One out of every eight people will experience at least a short disability during their working lives, and one out of every seven employees will be disabled for five years or more before retirement. Forty-eight percent of all home foreclosures are the result of a disability. Moreover, during the course of your career, you are three and a half times more likely to be injured and need disability coverage than you are to die and need life insurance.

I recommend to everyone that they make a priority of finding out how much disability coverage, if any, is provided by their employer. This coverage can vary greatly, but a typical group disability benefit plan might cover 60 percent of your base pay before taxes. Will you be able to live on 60 percent of your salary? Furthermore, any earnings you receive through bonuses and commissions aren't considered part of your base pay. If, for instance, your salary is $80,000 and you typically get $20,000 a year in bonuses, your disability policy would only cover 60 percent of the

$80,000. So, instead of bringing in the $100,000 a year you and your family are accustomed to, you would be receiving $48,000 (60 percent of $80,000).

The main purpose of disability insurance is to replace months or even years of lost future income. Many people assume that Social Security will provide for them if they are sick or injured and cannot work. However, Social Security offers disability coverage within very limited parameters. It is only available if your disability lasts more than twelve months or leads to death. Moreover, it only pays benefits if you cannot perform any job. In contrast, private disability insurance begins when your doctor determines that you cannot perform a job that you have been trained to do. On personal policies, this is called "occupation coverage." Some policies have even broader coverage, offering an "own occupation" clause that assumes you are disabled if you cannot perform the duties of your specific job. The cost and availability of disability insurance is usually determined by occupation. Just as a young nonsmoker is a lower risk to a life insurance company, an accountant who sits behind a desk is a lower risk than a roofer.

Here are a few more important concepts you should understand when investigating disability insurance.

Term of benefits. A key component to any policy is the length of time it will pay benefits. Some are designed to pay for as little as two years and then stop. Others are designed to pay until retirement age. Obviously the longer your benefit period, the higher the policy premiums will be.

Elimination period. A standard feature of disability insurance, this is the amount of time before you qualify for benefits. It can be as short as thirty days or as long as one year. A longer elimination period translates into lower premiums.

Noncancelable. This provision means that the insurance company can neither cancel your policy nor raise your premiums unless it stops writing coverage for everyone with your job classification. I advise that you buy only a noncancelable policy.

Because many large insurance companies offer disability insurance, be sure to shop around or consult with your insurance agent.

Conclusion

While it may seem overwhelming to try to create a complete financial plan that extends beyond tomorrow or next year or the year after, what better time is there than now? Moreover, once you look deeply at the cost of college, you understand that it will impact every other aspect of your financial life, most of all, your retirement.

Of course, just reaching retirement is not the finish line. Life expectancy keeps increasing, and people are living longer and longer, a trend not expected to reverse any time soon. A man who is sixty-five today has a 25 percent chance of living to ninety-two. A man who is eighty-five today has a 25 percent chance of living eleven years more. For married couples who are both sixty-five and older, there is a good chance that at least one member of the couple will live to nearly one hundred. That's a lot of years to need retirement income. It is why you need to handle your day-to-day finances efficiently, save money for retirement, and manage your investments properly even while you pay for college.

Returning to the theme of this book: If you are fifty years old and plan on retiring in fifteen years, what will $10,000 saved in college expenses do for you? That money invested today and compounded annually at 10 percent will provide you with another $41,772 for retirement. But perhaps you can do better: $50,000 saved in college expenses would provide you with an additional $208,862 for retirement.

Take a step back and give this major expense some thought. Unless you are among the extremely wealthy, how and what you pay for college will have a profound impact on your financial future.

Resources

Recommended Reading

Books on College Planning

The A's and B's of Academic Scholarships: 100,000 Scholarships for Top Students, Twenty-Sixth Edition by Anna Leider (Alexandria, VA : Octameron Assoc., 2007)

Fiske Guide to Colleges by Edward B. Fiske (Naperville, IL: Sourcebooks, Inc., 2007)

The Gatekeepers, Inside the Admissions Process of a Premier College by Jacques Steinberg (New York, NY: Penguin Group, 2003)

How to Go to College Almost for Free by Ben Kaplan (New York, NY: Collins, 2001)

Savingforcollege.com's Family Guide to College Savings by Joseph F. Hurley (Pittsford, NY: Savingforcollege.com, LLC, 2006)

Winning the College Admissions Game: Strategies for Parents & Students by Peter Van Buskirk (Lawrenceville, NJ: Peter son's, 2007)

Books on Retirement Planning

The Automatic Millionaire: A Powerful One-Step Plan to Live and Finish Rich by David Bach (New York, NY: Broadway, 2003)

Millionaire Next Door: The Surprising Secrets of America's Wealthy by Thomas J. Stanley and William D. Danko (New York, NY: Pocket, 2000)

Ordinary People, Extraordinary Wealth: The 8 Secrets of How 5,000 Ordinary Americans Became Successful Investors—and How You Can Too by Ric Edelman (New York, NY: Collins, 2000)

The Total Money Makeover: A Proven Plan for Financial Fitness, Second Edition, by Dave Ramsey (Nashville, TN: Thomas Nelson, 2000)

The Wealthy Barber, Updated: Everyone's Commonsense Guide to Becoming Financially Independent, Third Edition, by David Chilton (Roseville, CA: Prima Publishing, 1997)

Books on Investing

*The Dick Davis Dividend: Straight Talk on Making Money from 40
Years on Wall Street* by Dick Davis (Hoboken, NJ: Wiley, 2007)

*The Intelligent Asset Allocator: How to Build Your Portfolio to Maxi-
mize Returns and Minimize Risk* by William Bernstein (New
York, NY: McGraw-Hill, 2000)

The Little Book That Beats the Market by Joel Greenblatt (Hoboken, NJ: Wiley, 2005)

*The Little Book That Makes You Rich: A Proven Market-Beating
Formula for Growth Investing* by Louis Navellier (Hoboken,
NJ: Wiley, 2007)

The Only Investment Guide You'll Ever Need by Andrew Tobias
(Orlando, FL: Harcourt, 2005)

*A Random Walk Down Wall Street: The Time-Tested Strategy for
Successful Investing, Ninth Edition*, by Burton G. Malkiel (New
York, NY: W. W. Norton, 2007)

Online Resources

Acceptance Chances

College Admissions Services, Inc. (www.go4college.com), use
discount code: th1055

Campus Video Tours

theU.com (www.theU.com)

Collegiate Choice (www.CollegiateChoice.com)

Career Planning

Career Dimensions®, Inc. (www.focuscareer.com)

CollegeBoard.com, Inc. (www.myroad.collegeboard.com)

Lunch-Money.com, Inc. (www.collegetoolkit.com)

College Data

CollegeBoard.com, Inc. (www.collegeboard.com)

College Planning Assistance

American Institute of Certified Educational Planners
(www.aicep.org)

Certified Financial Planner Board of Standards, Inc.
(www.cfp.net)

Independent Educational Consultants Association
(www.IECAonline.com)

National Institute of Certified College Planners
(www.niccp.com)

College Savings

Bankrate.com (www.savingforcollege.com)

College Savings Bank (www.collegesavings.com)

SavingsBonds.com (www.savingsbonds.com)

TIAA-CREF Tuition Financing, Inc.

(www.independent529plan.org)

College Search

CollegeBoard.com, Inc. (collegeboard.com)

Lunch-Money.com, Inc. (www.collegetoolkit.com)

Peterson's (www.petersons.com)

Commercial Property Evaluation

FinAid.org (www.finaid.org)

Exam Credits

CollegeBoard.com, Inc. (www.collegeboard.com)

International Baccalaureate Organization (www.ibo.org)

Prometric™ DSST (www.getcollegecredit.com)

Expected Family Contribution Calculators

CollegeBoard.com, Inc. (www.myroad.collegeboard.com)

Lunch-Money.com, Inc. (www.collegetoolkit.com)

FinAid.org (www.finaid.org)

Financial Aid Forms

Free Application for Federal Student Aid (www.fafsa.ed.gov)

CSS/Financial Aid PROFILE* (www.profileonline.collegeboard.com)

Home Evaluations

FinAid.org (www.finaid.org)

MLS Network, Inc. (www.mls.com)

RealEstateABC.com (www.RealEstateABC.com)

Zillow.com (www.zillow.com)

Insurance Calculators

All Options Insurance (www.insurance.alloptions.com)

Yahoo! Finance (www.finance.yahoo.com)

Investing

CCH (www.finance.cch.com)

InvestorPlace Media, LLC (www.getrichwithgrowth.com)

MSN Money (www.moneycentral.msn.com)

Yahoo! Finance (www.finance.yahoo.com)

Merit-Based Scholarships

Peterson's (www.petersons.com)

Private Scholarships

CollegeBoard.com, Inc. (www.collegeboard.com)

FastWeb, LLC (www.fastweb.com)

Lunch-Money.com, Inc. (www.collegetoolkit.com)

Peterson's (www.petersons.com)

ScholarshipExperts.com (www.scholarshipexperts.com)

Retirement Calculator

Bankrate.com (www.bankrate.com)

Test Preparation

Peterson's (www.petersons.com)

PrepMe, Inc. (www.prepme.com)

Index

Books from Bay Tree Publishing

www.BayTreePublish.com

A Patient's Guide to Chinese Medicine

Dr. Shen's Handbook of Herbs and Acupuncture

by Joel Harvey Schreck

Chinese herbal medicines are increasingly popular as alternative medical therapies and are now available everywhere in the country. This book, a "patient's guide," provides an A-to-Z list of herbal remedies by ailment. The detailed information on herbal properties, preparation, dosage, and effectiveness make this an easy-to-use handbook for getting optimum help from traditional Chinese herbs and practices.

Joel Harvey Schreck, L.Ac. (aka Dr. Shen) is a licensed acupuncturist with more than twenty years in private practice. His popular "Dr. Shen" line of herbs is sold in natural foods stores, including large chains, and online.

$18.95, paperback, 288 pages 6" X 9" ISBN: 978-0-9801758-0-6

Get Slightly Famous, 2nd Edition

Become a Celebrity in Your Field and Attract More Business with Less Effort

by Steven Van Yoder

With practical marketing help for the small business owner or independent professional on every page, *Get Slightly Famous*™ shows how any business owner can break out of the sea of competing look-alikes to become "slightly famous." This expanded new edition provides a toolbox of strategies for:

- Getting media attention
- Becoming a center of influence in your industry
- Leveraging the Internet and Web 2.0
- Creating ancillary "info-products" that supplement your income and build public awareness.

Steven Van Yoder is a PR practitioner and freelance journalist whose work has appeared in more than 200 publications.

"*Get Slightly Famous* is more than just slightly valuable, more than just slightly fun to read, and more than just slightly wonderful. It is loaded with insights I wish I had when I was first starting out. But I'm delighted to get them now, and I'll bet every reader will feel the same."
  —**Jay Conrad Levinson**, author of the "Guerrilla Marketing" series

"With practical ideas and inspirational success stories, this is a must-read for entrepreneurs. The book's underlying premise and promotional strategies will make readers both more memorable and more money."
  —**PR Week**

$18.95 paperback, 324 pages, 6" X 9" ISBN: 0-9720021-7-2

Losing the Way

A Memoir of Spiritual Longing, Manipulation, Abuse, and Escape

by Kristen Skedgell

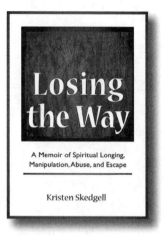

A riveting and finely crafted true story, *Losing the Way* recounts how the daughter of East Coast intellectuals was recruited into a well-known right-wing Bible cult, The Way International, where she was manipulated, betrayed, and abused. In the end, she was rescued by the "worldly" mother she rejected. Skedgell shows how easily an idealistic young person can be swept away by a spiritual quest, and she skillfully exposes the quiet malevolence lurking beneath the religious exterior of a false leader.

Kristen Skedgell is a Clinical Social Worker at a maximum-security correctional facility.

"How is it that a woman determined to be good—virtuous—can make such an unholy mess of her life? In pursuit of grace, Kristen Skedgell gave herself to one devil after another. She lost her way in life, but not on the page, and her account of finding her way back home, back to the self she denied and betrayed, has something to teach all of us."
  —**Kathryn Harrison**, author of *The Kiss*

"Kristen Skedgell helps us to see the true power of love and faith. She reminds us of what it means to be genuinely connected to one another and our capacity to thrive after being lost."
  —**Frederick J. Streets**, former Chaplain of Yale University; Professor in Pastoral Counseling, Wurzweiler School of Social Work, Yeshiva University; Associate Professor Pastoral Theology, Yale Divinity School

$18.95 paperback, 288 pages, 6" X 9" ISBN: 978-9720021-9-6

Them and Us
Cult Thinking and the Terrorist Threat

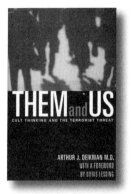

by Arthur J. Deikman, M.D.
Foreword by Doris Lessing

Them and Us shows the connection between classic cult manipulation and the milder forms of group pressure that can be found in churches and schools, mainstream political movements and corporate boardrooms. In her foreword, Doris Lessing discusses the ways that cult thinking affects contemporary society.

Arthur J. Deikman, M.D. is a professor of psychiatry at the University of California, San Francisco

$17.95 paperback, 240 pages, 6" X 9" ISBN: 0-9720021-2-X

Take Back Your Life
Recovering from Cults and Abusive Relationships

by Janja Lalich and
Madeleine Landau Tobias

Cult victims and those who have suffered abusive relationships often suffer from fear, confusion, low-self esteem, and post-traumatic stress. *Take Back Your Life* explains the seductive draw that leads people into such situations, provides insightful information for assessing what happened, and hands-on tools for getting back on track. Written for the victims, their families, and professionals, this book leads readers through the healing process.

Janja Lalich, Ph.D., is Associate Professor of Sociology at California State University, Chico. **Madeleine Tobias, M.S., R.N., C.S.**, is the Clinical Coordinator and a psychotherapist at the Vet Center in White River Junction, Vermont.

$19.50 paperback, 376 pages, 6" X 9" ISBN: 0-9720021-5-4

Saving Energy, Growing Jobs

How Environmental Protection Promotes Economic Growth, Profitability, Innovation, and Competition

by David B. Goldstein
Foreword by Senator Olympia J. Snowe

Saving Energy, Growing Jobs shows that well-conceived environmental regulations create more jobs, lead to more efficient designs, and provide less expensive products. It offers a new paradigm for the economy and the environment in which the nation (and the world) can preserve its resources and promote prosperity at the same time. This ground-breaking book:

- Profiles the unexpected success of early energy regulations
- Shows how markets actually work and how they fail
- Exposes both the myths of environmentalists and anti-environmentalists
- Provides a model for well-designed environmental policies
- Offers guidelines for transforming the current political debate

Proposing that environmental protection can drive innovation, Goldstein outlines incentives and regulations that can speed the process.

David B. Goldstein, Ph.D., is Energy Program Director for the Natural Resources Defense Council and a MacArthur ("genius award") Fellow. His contribution to energy efficiency standards for appliances is estimated to save as much energy every year as the entire output of the U.S. nuclear energy program.

"David Goldstein provides us with a compelling combination of facts and analysis that all point to one truth: environment and business have never been more compatible. *Saving Energy, Growing Jobs* is a must-read regardless where you reside on the political spectrum."
—**Senator Dianne Feinstein**

"If we are to succeed in tackling the most urgent of our environmental problems, businesses and environmentalists need to work together. David Goldstein has written the definitive work on how to make it happen."
—**Robert J. Fisher**, Chairman of the Board, Gap Inc.

$18.95 paperback, 336 pages, 6" X 9" ISBN: 0-9720021-6-2

Get Hired Now!™

A 28-Day Program for Landing the Job You Want

by C.J. Hayden and Frank Traditi
Foreword by Wendy S. Enelow

In a world where 85 percent of available jobs are never advertised, *Get Hired Now!* provides hands-on techniques to help job-seekers tap into the hidden job market. This inspirational and motivational book shows how to take advantage of the single most important factor in a successful job search, the power of personal relationships. At the heart of the book, a systematic, structured 28-day program helps readers identify job search strategies, determine the next important step, and stay motivated in the face of frustration and rejection.

C.J. Hayden is a Master Certified Coach and author of the bestselling *Get Clients Now!™*. Since 1992 she has helped thousands of professionals achieve career success.

Frank Traditi is a career strategist and executive coach with more than 20 years of experience in management, sales, and marketing for Fortune 500 companies, including MCI, Inc.

"This book will literally lead you by the hand and walk you through 28 days of what you should do in order to succeed. A treasure trove of practical, tested ideas."
   —**Dr. Stephen R. Covey,** author, *The 7 Habits of Highly Effective People* and *The 8th Habit: From Effectiveness to Greatness*

"... has lessons on how to pitch yourself, answer tough interview questions and get around the HR department."
—**San Francisco Examiner**

$17.95 paperback, 336 pages, 6" X 9" ISBN: 0-9720021-3-8

The Case for Affirmative Action in University Admissions

by Bob Laird

Foreword by the Rev. Jesse L. Jackson

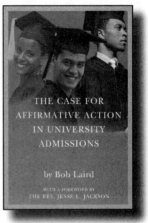

While two recent Supreme Court decisions have insured that affirmative action will continue to play a central role in creating equal educational opportunities for minority students, the future of that policy is precarious and the stakes high. This book explains the critical role of affirmative action in creating diverse public institutions, describes the turbulent debates regarding such programs, and clarifies the guidelines that will govern affirmative action policies in education in the immediate future.

Bob Laird was Director of Undergraduate Admission at the University of California, Berkeley for six years, and an admissions professional for twenty-five years. He has worked in the eye of the storm surrounding admissions and social policy issues.

"… explores the basic questions and concerns surrounding the challenge of balancing the need for greater diversity against notions of a color-blind society … Laird offers clear recommendations for admissions policy makers …"
   —Booklist

"… one of the best defenses of affirmative action in university admissions that anyone has ever written."
   —Nicholas Lemann, Dean of the Graduate School of Journalism at
      Columbia University and author of *The Big Test: The Secret History of
      the American Meritocracy*

$26.95 hardcover, 288 pages, 6" X 9" ISBN: 0-9720021-4-6

"As college costs continue to skyrocket, it is crucial that parents and grandparents become educated savers and consumers. Tim Higgins' savings and cost-cutting options coupled with his ability to understand the total financial picture is extremely valuable."
  —Gregg Cohen, President, CampusBound.com

"In the 16 years I have been guiding students and parents through the college selection and admissions process, I have rarely come across a financial planner like Tim Higgins. His timely and topical book is filled with legitimate money-saving strategies and sound recommendations."
  —Eric Goodhart, Director, SmartCollegePlanning.org

"Tim Higgins is unique in his field of college financial planning in that he truly understands the concerns families have about this huge investment, and he views the process holistically. Although college is a critical step for your child's future, your own financial viability is also important. Tim demystifies the financial planning process and ensures that your whole family is served. This book is the roadmap to maximizing your financial potential."
  —Charlotte Klaar, Director, College Consulting Services

"Affording college has become increasingly more difficult especially for the middle class. The cost of attending college and how to finance that investment are becoming increasingly more important factors when choosing a school. Tim Higgins gives excellent advice for how to most efficiently pay for college."
  —Timothy B. Lee, Ed.M., Certified Educational Planner, AHP Educational Consulting, and President of the Independent Educational Consultants Association